Credo

Ray Pritchard

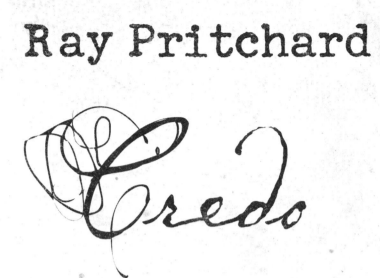

Credo

Believing in Something to Die For

CROSSWAY BOOKS

A PUBLISHING MINISTRY OF
GOOD NEWS PUBLISHERS
WHEATON, ILLINOIS

Credo

Copyright © 2005 by Ray Pritchard

Published by Crossway Books
  a publishing ministry of Good News Publishers
  1300 Crescent Street
  Wheaton, Illinois 60187

Cover design: Josh Dennis

First printing, 2005

Printed in the United States of America

Library of Congress Cataloging-in-Publication Data
Pritchard, Ray, 1952-
 Credo : believing in something to die for / Ray Pritchard.
  p. cm.
 ISBN 13: 978-1-58134-719-7 (tpb)
 ISBN 10: 1-58134-719-7
 1. Apostles' Creed. I. Title.
BT993.3.P75 2005
238'.11—dc22   2005018386

RRDH		17	16	15	14	13	12	11	10	09	08	07
15	14	13	12	11	10	9	8	7	6	5	4	3	2

To
TOM AND CAROL
MIKE AND BETSI
TOM AND FAY
*who understand
the true meaning
of friendship*

Contents

Acknowledgments

I am grateful to Marvin Padgett who first had the vision for this project. Bill Jensen helped sharpen my focus, and Ted Griffin exercised enormous patience while waiting for this manuscript to be finished so he could begin editing it. I am thankful also to Lane, Ebeth, and Geoff Dennis for their continued encouragement and support. I have been privileged to serve as pastor of Calvary Memorial Church in Oak Park, Illinois, since 1989. The congregation journeyed with me through the Apostles' Creed over a six-month period in 2004. Their prayers sustained me as we studied the Creed together. Finally, I am thankful for my wife, Marlene, and to my three sons—Josh, Mark, and Nick. No man could ask for a better family.

When William Barclay wrote on the Apostles' Creed, he noted his debt to the multitudes who have written on the Creed over the centuries. I share in that debt, and I will be glad if this book helps ground a new generation in the essential truths of the Christian faith.

THE APOSTLES' CREED

I believe in God, the Father Almighty,
the Creator of heaven and earth,
and in Jesus Christ, his only Son, our Lord:
Who was conceived of the Holy Spirit,
born of the Virgin Mary,
suffered under Pontius Pilate,
was crucified, died, and was buried.
He descended into hell.
The third day he arose again from the dead.
He ascended into heaven
and sits at the right hand of God the Father Almighty,
whence he shall come to judge the living and the dead.
I believe in the Holy Spirit,
the holy catholic church,
the communion of saints,
the forgiveness of sins,
the resurrection of the body,
and life everlasting.
Amen.

Introduction

I can think of several reasons why we need to study the Apostles' Creed.

GOOD THEOLOGY CAN SAVE YOUR LIFE

We all know that good theology can save your soul, but in a time of trouble, if you know and remember the truth, what you know and remember can save you from despair. During an interview on a radio station in Dallas, we took a call from a woman who was going through a hard time in her marriage, with her health, and with some family relationships. As I listened, I realized she was a Christian who felt overwhelmed. I knew I couldn't solve her problems in two minutes. So I told her that she needed to go back to the first principles and remind herself of those things she knew to be true. "Good theology can save your life," I told her. What "first principles" are we talking about? Here's a short list:

- God is good.
- God is faithful.
- He will never leave me.
- His mercy endures forever.
- What's happening to me is not a mistake.
- God has a purpose.
- He is working out his plan for me.
- God still loves me.
- The Holy Spirit indwells me.
- Jesus is alive today.
- He will return to earth for his people someday.

Credo

Before a worship service one Sunday, I chatted with a friend I hadn't seen for many months. He and his wife had been through a series of incredibly difficult experiences over the previous two or three years. Although he had no idea what I would be preaching on, he grabbed my hand and said, "Tell the people that God is faithful. Tell them those three words: *God is faithful*." Then he added, "I haven't always been faithful, but God has been faithful to me." Good theology saves you from despair when hard times come.

OUR CHRISTIAN FAITH MUST BE FOUNDED ON TRUTH

In 1923 J. Gresham Machen wrote a groundbreaking book called *Christianity and Liberalism* in which he demonstrated the fundamental difference between biblical Christianity and liberal Christianity. Near the end of the first chapter, he explains the importance of truth to the Christian faith:

> Christianity is based, then, upon an account of something that happened, and the Christian worker is primarily a witness. But if so, it is rather important that the Christian worker should tell the truth. When a man takes his seat upon the witness stand, it makes little difference what the cut of his coat is, or whether his sentences are nicely turned. The important thing is that he tell the truth, the whole truth, and nothing but the truth.[1]

Today many people who claim to know Jesus don't believe that the Bible is the Word of God. I want to help people find a personal relationship with the Christ revealed in the Bible. Salvation is life-changing precisely because it is based on the truth.

TRUE FAITH RESTS ON THE PRINCIPLE OF AUTHORITY

If you think about it, Christians believe something very profound and radical. In an age of moral and spiritual anarchy, we believe there is a

God in heaven who has spoken to the human race, and he has not stuttered. He has made himself clear in his Word, the Bible. Writing in the Manchester (England) *Guardian*, Christina Odone nails this down:

> We believe in authority. In an era that prizes individual freedom, Christians believe in a supreme being who dictates our words and deeds. To modern ears, the concept sounds outrageously autocratic. From when to die to when to give birth, from whom to have sex with, to how to spend their money, the chatteratis believe they should enjoy unlimited freedom. But for the Christian, freedom is not an end in itself. Unfettered individualism can mean greed and selfishness, the evasion of personal responsibility, the destruction of the family. Christians believe that from an all-powerful authority stems a clear system of judgment which teaches that there is a right and a wrong.[2]

The church must once again declare the truth of God with boldness. To a world that rejects authority, the church must declare the authority of God. The world says, "We want freedom." God says, "If you want freedom, obey my Word." Today the world follows the false trinity of tolerance, diversity, and pluralism. Our task is to proclaim the truth of God even to those who reject it because that is what sets men free.

SPIRITUAL GROWTH DOES NOT HAPPEN BY ACCIDENT

"Build yourselves up in your most holy faith" (Jude 20). We see here *the sacred nature of the Christian faith*. Our faith is "holy" because it comes from a holy God. We do not have the right to change the Christian faith just because we find it uncomfortable or unpopular. We are to take our faith seriously because it comes from a holy God.

Secondly, *spiritual growth is not optional*. Every Christian is called to grow in God's grace, his undeserved kindness toward us (2 Peter

3:18). Ephesians 4:15 tells us to "grow up in every way into him who is the head, into Christ," and Colossians 2:7 says that we are to be "rooted and built up in him and established in the faith." God expects us to grow in grace. A year from now, we ought to be further along in our spiritual journey than we are today.

Most people make some sort of fitness-related resolution each January. Maybe you're tired of carrying extra pounds and having your clothes not fit. Maybe you have decided to get in shape physically. Even though I'm no expert in this area and I don't have any fitness videos to sell, I know this: If you're going to lose weight this year, you can't keep on doing what you've been doing. If you don't make a change, you'll still be overweight and out of shape twelve months from now.

The same is true if you want to grow spiritually. At some point you have to change your schedule and rearrange your priorities. That may mean getting up earlier so you have time to read the Bible and pray. It may mean joining a Bible study group or getting involved in a teaching ministry to children or visiting prisoners or volunteering at a local pro-life center. We are commanded to build ourselves up in our most holy faith, but spiritual growth is not magic. It requires a serious commitment from us or it won't happen.

WE OWE IT TO THE WORLD, TO OURSELVES, AND TO OUR GOD

Romans 12:2 tells us not to be conformed to the world. We must not let the world squeeze us into its mold.

We need Christians who will stand out because they don't go with the flow.

But that verse also tells us *how* to be radical nonconformists. We are "transformed" by the "renewal" of our minds. Spiritual growth begins in the mind as we learn the truths of God. Then we are ready to show the world who Jesus is.

That's where the Apostles' Creed comes in. As the oldest statement of Christian faith outside the Bible, it deserves our close attention.

Because it is recognized by all branches of the Christian faith, it offers a foundation of Christian unity that transcends denominational differences. Because it is both brief and concise, it offers us a broad outline of all the major areas of Christian doctrine. In this book we're going to consider it slowly, phrase by phrase, sometimes even word by word.

The moral and spiritual confusion of these days offers an incredible opportunity to the church of Jesus Christ. If the people of this generation do not find God's truth, they will believe Satan's lie. After all, a starving dog will eat whatever you put in front of him. Something has to fill the void within. And that means we have a great opportunity. It's not enough to simply protect our children. It's not enough to learn what is true and what is false. We have an obligation that goes beyond the walls of our churches and beyond our own families. God has made us debtors to the whole world. It won't be enough in the Last Day to say, "But, Lord, I took care of my family. I told them about you. See, we're all here." The Lord will say back to us, "My child, what did you do for your friends and neighbors? What about that man who came to your door? What about your sister, your daddy, your boss, your pals at work? Did you even try to tell them about me?"

We live in the greatest days of human history. It may well be that we are the final generation before the return of Christ. That would explain why Satan has made such an energetic effort to spread his lies. A battle is going on between God and Satan. But where sin abounds, grace super-abounds. The very fact that we live in such spiritual darkness means that when the light shines, *it really shines*. Don't be discouraged by the difficulty of the task. Instead be encouraged by the opportunities of this hour. Our task to is to know what we believe so that, being grounded ourselves, we have something of eternal value to share with others. If that sounds exciting to you, turn the page and let's get started.

1

You Are What You Believe: Why the Apostles' Creed Matters

If you confess with your mouth that Jesus is Lord and believe in your heart that God raised him from the dead, you will be saved. For with the heart one believes and is justified, and with the mouth one confesses and is saved.

ROMANS 10:9-10

Why bother with the Apostles' Creed?

There are three good answers to that question. First, *it is the oldest and most widely accepted creed*, recognized by all branches of Christianity—Protestant, Catholic, and Orthodox. For two thousand years it has served as a succinct statement of the irreducible minimum of the Christian faith. Second, *it offers a broad survey of Christian doctrine.* It starts with creation and ends with eternal life. That's about as broad as you can get. As we will see, it is not comprehensive, but everything it covers is important. If you want to go back to basics, this is a good place to begin. Third, *the Creed offers a radical challenge to the skepticism of this generation.* The people of the world doubt that we can be certain about anything. Over against that uncertainty we have the first two words of the Creed: "I believe," and that is good for the soul.[3]

THE NECESSITY OF THE APOSTLES' CREED

The key phrase of the book of Judges, although written over three thousand years ago, could have been written last week: "Everyone did what

Credo

was right in his own eyes" (21:25). It would be hard to find a more fitting description of modern American life. If you ask people on the street what they believe, you will receive a bewildering array of answers. Consider this quote from a twenty-something backpacker in Boston when asked what he believed: "I believe there's some Higher Power, I think. But I don't know. Like right now I'm at a point where I don't know what to believe, but I'm open to everything. So I like to believe in everything, because I don't know what it is I truly believe in." That strikes me as a totally honest statement, and I think he speaks for a whole generation.

No "Bible Thumpers"

If we ask people on the street how they determine what they believe, almost everyone will point to their opinions or feelings and say, "This is my best guess." Feelings trump everything else nowadays. A friend sent me the following e-mail:

> My brother recently announced that he was now engaged to a woman he met on a "Christian" Internet dating service. During our dinner conversation he told me all about her and said that one of his qualifications for a wife was that she had to have Christian beliefs, but not act like a "Bible thumper." He explained this statement by saying that he wanted a woman who believed in Christian values but not necessarily someone who was a Christian and lived out her faith.
>
> I asked him what his views were on Christianity and he replied that he was a Christian and believed that Jesus died on the cross for our sins. He went on to say that he agreed with all the findings of the "Jesus Seminar." Among other things, he said he believed that Christ was not born of a virgin, he did not physically rise from the dead, and that there was nothing wrong with gay pastors. I asked him what he based his beliefs on and he explained that they were based on his own understanding of who God is.

That strikes me as a fairly convenient religion. You keep the parts of the Bible you like, and you get to throw away the rest. This is one reason why we desperately need the Apostles' Creed.

The Creed stands as an important corrective to the me-centered theology of the present day.

The Creed reminds us that there are boundaries to the Christian faith—not everything is negotiable. Some things *must* be believed if you are to call yourself a Christian. You can choose to live outside those boundaries, but if you do, you aren't living as a Christian, and you shouldn't call yourself one.

Not everything is negotiable. Some things must be believed if you are to call yourself a Christian.

This leads us to a vital truth point: *Christianity is a doctrinal faith.* You can't just fill it in with whatever content you desire. Christianity is a life based on the doctrines of the Bible. We must never say, "As long as you believe in Jesus, it doesn't matter what else you believe." Unless the Jesus we believe in is the Christ of the Bible, he's not the real Jesus at all.

This means that Christianity is more than a conversion experience.

There are things to learn, and there are doctrines we are required to believe. That's why the Apostles' Creed is so important in the history of the church. Truth is not up for grabs, and it is not decided by what we feel or by a majority vote or by the latest opinion poll. The Creed reminds us that truth comes from God, and that is where we must start in our spiritual journey.

THE HISTORY OF THE APOSTLES' CREED

The word *creed* comes from the Latin word *credo*, which means, "I believe." Originally the Apostles' Creed was not a formal, written document. It began, in the earliest days of the Christian church, as a baptismal formula. Whenever I perform a baptism, I always ask each person four questions before I baptize him or her:
- "Do you believe that Jesus Christ is the Son of God?"
- "Do you believe that Jesus died on the cross and rose from the dead?"

- "Are you trusting Jesus Christ and him alone as your Lord and Savior?"
- "And do you wish to be baptized and live for him?"

I ask the candidates to speak loudly so the congregation knows why they are being baptized. Their answers form the public profession of faith that precedes their baptism. If a candidate ever refuses to answer or if the answer is incorrect (that hasn't happened yet in all the years I've been a pastor), I will not baptize him or her. That's how important those questions are.

Early Christians followed a similar practice, but their questions were slightly different. Evidently they asked questions like:

- "Do you believe in God the Father Almighty, Maker of Heaven and Earth?"
- "Do you believe in Jesus Christ, God's Son, our Lord?"
- "Do you believe Christ died on the cross and rose again from the dead?"

From those early questions the Creed developed into its current form over many generations.[4]

The Word Comes First

Since this book is about the Apostles' Creed, I want to be clear up front that we don't base our faith on any creed or statement of faith.

Our ultimate source of authority is the written Word of God.

Because the Bible is inspired by God (2 Timothy 3:16), the Word is true in all its parts and is entirely trustworthy. No creed can make that claim for itself. Think of it this way: First there is God who gives us his Word. Then from the Word come the creeds and confessions of the church. The church believes the creeds and confessions because they reflect what God has said in his Word. This doesn't mean that everything found in every creed or confession is correct. But it does mean that creeds and confessions of faith are helpful as long as they reflect what the Word of God actually says.

Faith is not a coin that you put into a vending machine, so that if you put in enough you will get what you want from God. Faith is the empty hand of a beggar reaching out to receive the gift of a king. (Rodney A. Stortz, DANIEL: THE TRIUMPH OF GOD'S KINGDOM)

THE IMPORTANCE OF THE APOSTLES' CREED

Let's begin with six fast facts about the Creed: First, as we've seen, *it is very old*. Scholars believe that its earliest form can be traced back to A.D. 120. Second, surprisingly, *it was not written by the apostles*. It is called the Apostles' Creed because it summarizes what the apostles taught. Third, *it is brief*. Most English translations contain 110-120 words. Fourth, *it is God-centered*. In fact, it is Trinitarian. The first thought deals with God the Father, the second with God the Son, the third with God the Holy Spirit. Fifth, *it is selective*. The Creed touches on the central issues of the Christian faith, but there is much it passes over. It says nothing about Satan, angels, demons, predestination, baptism, church government, or the details of Christ's future Second Coming. Sixth, *it is easy to memorize*.

Here's a handy way to think about the Creed. Let's suppose that before you leave on vacation you purchase a book of maps to help you find your way. That book of maps contains separate maps for all fifty states, and there will be smaller inset maps for all of the larger cities in each state. At the front of the book there is a large, two-page map of the United States. If you live in the Los Angeles area and you want to drive from Downey to La Habra, the U.S. map won't do you any good. And the state map won't help much either. You'll need to consult a map of Los Angeles. But if you want to drive from Miami to Seattle, you'll keep the book open to the map of the entire United States. The Apostles' Creed is like that large map. It gives you the big picture of what Christians believe. We believe more than what the Creed says, but we don't believe less than that.

If you've read this far, you may wonder, "What does all this have to do with me?" Good question. After all, we live in a practical age when people want to know how the truth impacts them personally. The answer is found in the first two words of the Creed: "I believe." That's a very powerful assertion. It's not the same as saying, "I know" or "I think" or "I feel."

To say, "I believe" means that you are making a personal commitment to the truth.

Romans 1:16 declares that the gospel is "the power of God" that brings "salvation to everyone who believes." And Romans 10:9-10 adds the concept of believing "in your heart," which means to believe from the depths of your being. That's why the Gospel of John declares more than eighty times that salvation comes to those who believe. In a deep sense, you are what you believe.

What you believe determines your destiny.

John 3:16 tells us that God gave his Son so that whoever believes in him would not perish but have everlasting life. Your eternal destiny depends on whether or not you believe in Jesus "in your heart."

What It Means to Say "I Believe"

The Greek word translated "believe" in the New Testament is *pisteuo*, which means to "believe into" something or someone. Now, if I say, "I believe it's going to rain tomorrow," that's nothing more than a hunch. If I say, "I believe George Washington was the first President of the United States," that refers to a settled historical fact. But if I say, "I believe in Jesus with all my heart," I have made a different sort of statement altogether.

Suppose a doctor tells me, "I'm sorry, but you have cancer that is life-threatening. Chemotherapy can kill the cancer, but it is likely to make you sick. But if you're willing to take it, you can be cured." In that case, to say, "I believe in my doctor" means something very specific. It doesn't mean "I believe he really is a doctor" or "I believe he's right when he says I have cancer" or even "I believe the chemotherapy can cure me." You don't truly believe in your doctor until you roll up your sleeve and let that life-saving medicine enter your veins. To believe in your doctor means to trust yourself completely to his care, accept his diagnosis, and put your life in his hands.

Believing in Jesus means to trust him completely with your eternal destiny.

It means to trust Christ so completely that if he can't take you to heaven, you aren't going to go there.

CHARLES BLONDIN

In the nineteenth century the greatest tightrope walker in the world was a man named Charles Blondin. On June 30, 1859, he became the first man in history to walk on a tightrope across Niagara Falls. Over twenty-five thousand people gathered to watch him walk 1,100 feet suspended on a tiny rope 160 feet above the raging waters. He worked without a net or safety harness of any kind. The slightest slip would prove fatal. When he safely reached the Canadian side of the Falls, the crowd burst into a mighty roar. In the days that followed he walked across the Falls many times. Once he walked across on stilts. Another time he took a chair and a stove with him and sat down midway across, cooked an omelette, and ate it. Once he carried his manager across riding piggyback.

On one occasion he asked the cheering spectators if they thought he could push a man across in a wheelbarrow. A mighty roar of approval rose from the crowd. Spying a man cheering loudly, he asked, "Sir, do you think I could safely carry you across in this wheelbarrow?" "Yes, of course." "Then get in," the Great Blondin replied with a smile. The man refused.

It's one thing to believe a man can walk across by himself. It's another thing to believe he could safely carry someone across. But it's something else entirely to get into the wheelbarrow yourself. Believing in Jesus is like getting into the wheelbarrow. It's entrusting all that you are to all that he is.

Believing in Jesus is entrusting all that you are to all that he is.

Credo

I spoke with a man whose father died recently. Although his father went to church and often heard about Jesus, the son worried about his father's salvation. I reminded the man that it's not the *amount* of faith that matters; it's the *object* of faith that makes all the difference. Weak faith in a strong object matters more than strong faith in a weak object.

It's not a matter of how much you believe—what's important is whether or not you are trusting the Lord Jesus Christ to save you.

In 2 Timothy 1:12 Paul says, "I know *whom* I have believed." As Spurgeon puts it, it is as if he says, "I know the person into whose hand I have committed my present condition, and my eternal destiny. I know who he is, and I therefore, without any hesitation, leave myself in his hands. It is the beginning of spiritual life to believe Jesus Christ."[5] You cannot keep yourself safe. Your only hope is to entrust all that you are and have to Jesus.

A few years ago I used the following illustration in one of my books. Three frogs are sitting on a log. Two of them decide to jump off. How many are left on the log? All three of them. Deciding to jump is not the same thing as actually jumping. A man in prison read that illustration and wrote to tell me how much it had impacted his life. Until then he had many times decided to believe in Jesus. But as long as you are just deciding, you haven't believed yet.

One final word. The Apostles' Creed begins with the words "I believe." Why doesn't it say, "We believe"? The answer is simple. *True belief is always personal.* I can't believe for you, and you can't believe for me. You can't live on the faith of those around you.

At its heart, the church is a community of believers who are joined together by their shared faith in Jesus Christ.

That's why the church for two thousand years has affirmed the Apostles' Creed. It expresses our common faith in Christ. The Creed begins with two simple words: "I believe." Do you? No one can sit on the fence forever. Remember, a Christian is a person who truly believes in Jesus Christ. Do you? Eternity hangs on your answer.

THINK ABOUT IT!

1. Can a two-thousand-year-old creed really have meaning for us today? Why or why not? What are the specific values of the Apostles' Creed?

2. Do you agree or disagree that Christianity is more than a conversion experience? What does it truly mean, according to the Bible, to be a Christian?

3. Why is what we believe so important? Have you personally believed in Jesus Christ as your Savior? What does this mean to you? What difference has it made in your life?

2

The Greatest Risk
You'll Ever Take:
"I Believe in God"

And without faith it is impossible to please him, for whoever
would draw near to God must believe that he exists and that
he rewards those who seek him.

HEBREWS 11:6

Either you believe in God or you don't.

If you do, then you are in good company. According to a recent Fox
News poll, 92 percent of those surveyed say they believe in God.[6] Most
people believe in God, even if they can't agree on what kind of God they
believe in. So it may seem unnecessary to devote a chapter to the first
phrase of the Apostles' Creed, "I believe in God." But it's always dangerous to take our faith for granted.

Let's unpack the phrase, "I believe in God" by breaking it down
into several statements.

A BASIC DECLARATION: GOD IS,
IS THE CENTRAL FACT OF THE UNIVERSE

The very first verse of the Bible establishes this truth in these majestic
and simple words: "In the beginning, God created the heavens and the
earth." Everything God wants us to know starts right here. This verse

is a declaration, not an argument. A few years ago E. V. Hill preached a powerful sermon at a Promise Keepers gathering in Chicago. In his own unforgettable style, he preached for forty minutes on just two words: "God is." He said it over and over again. He whispered it, and he shouted it. He illustrated it, declared it, proclaimed it, and dared anyone to deny it. Once you get it settled in your heart that "God is," a lot of other problems will be solved as well.

> Once you get it settled in your heart that "God is,"
> a lot of other problems will be solved as well.

A LOGICAL IMPLICATION: ALL THINGS OWE THEIR EXISTENCE TO GOD THE CREATOR

Because God is the Creator, he is also the owner of all things. If I make a toy boat, I can truly say, "I created it, and I own it." Since God made us, he can do with us as he pleases. That's not a popular topic in contemporary American life. We want to do our own thing, go our own way, live the way we want, do whatever we feel like doing whenever we want to do it. But since God created us, he owns us, and we are accountable to him for everything we say and do. That's not a happy thought for many people, but it's true nevertheless.

As is so often the case, we get some very good help on this point from dear old Martin Luther. Writing over 450 years ago, he comments, "I believe that God created me, along with all creatures. He gave to me: body and soul, eyes, ears and all the other parts of my body, my mind and all my senses and preserves them as well. He gives me clothing and shoes, food and drink, house and land, wife and children, fields, animals and all I own. Every day He abundantly provides everything I need to nourish this body and life. He protects me against all danger, shields and defends me from all evil. He does all this because of His pure, fatherly and divine goodness and His mercy, not because I've earned it or deserved it. For all of this, I must thank Him, praise Him, serve Him and obey Him. Yes, this is true!"[7] To which I say, right on, brother!

AN INESCAPABLE REVELATION:
THE TRUTH ABOUT GOD
HAS BEEN MADE KNOWN TO EVERYONE

This fact comes from Romans 1:19-20: "For what can be known about God is *plain to them*, because God has *shown it to them*. For his invisible attributes, namely, his eternal power and divine nature, have been *clearly perceived*, ever since the creation of the world, in the things that have been made. So they are *without excuse*" (emphasis added). Paul uses the word "plain" to describe God's revelation of himself to all mankind. Then in verse 20 he adds that the truth about God is "clearly perceived" in nature. We can say it this way:

Everyone knows there is a God, and the people who say they do not believe in God are deceiving themselves.

God created all that we see around us. He created the sun, the stars, the moon, and the planets. He created the comets and the asteroids. He created the quasars and the pulsars and the black holes of space. Scientists estimate there are four hundred billion stars in the Milky Way Galaxy, and they estimate there are more than one hundred billion galaxies, each with at least one hundred billion stars. Imagine that. And God hung each one in space and calls each one by name ("He determines the number of the stars; he gives to all of them their names," Psalm 147:4). No wonder the Bible says, "The heavens declare the glory of God, and the sky above proclaims his handiwork" (Psalm 19:1).

God has left his fingerprints all over the universe. You have to be blind not to see them. Suppose you visited my house while I was not there. How much could you learn about my family just from looking around? You might suspect we had boys from the basketball goal above the garage door. You would know that we love football from the picture of Mark in his uniform on the side of the refrigerator and from the autograph of Eli Manning in Nick's bedroom. Although you might not know I was a pastor, you would certainly know I often study the Bible from seeing all the Bibles and commentaries strewn around the computer in the corner of our dining room. In our bedroom you would find artifacts from our trips to the Holy Land. By counting the beds you would figure out that we probably have three boys. And if you looked in my closet, you'd discover I'm tall just by looking at my suits. In the end you'd know a lot about me although you wouldn't know me personally. The clues are everywhere for those who care to look.

As in a shell we listen to the murmurs of the sea, so in the intricacies of creation we hear the praises of God. (Charles Haddon Spurgeon, SPURGEON'S DAILY TREASURE FROM THE PSALMS)

This world is God's house. He's left clues everywhere about what kind of God he is. When you stand at the Grand Canyon, you can't help but be overwhelmed at the mighty power of God to create such magnificence. He must have had a mighty hand to scoop out the Royal Gorge in Colorado. The changing colors of the Great Smoky Mountains proclaim his creativity.

The galaxies shout out, "He is here." The wildflowers sing together, "He is here." The rippling brooks join in, "He is here." The birds sing it, the lions roar it, the fish write it in the oceans—"He is here." All creation joins to sing his praise. The heavens declare it, the earth repeats it, and the wind whispers it—"He is here." The mighty sequoia tells it to the eagle who soars overhead, and the lamb and the wolf agree, "He is here." God has left his fingerprints all over this world. Every rock, every twig, every river, and every mountain bears his signature.

That's the point of Romans 1: Everyone knows something about God! It doesn't matter whether they consciously think about it or not. The truth is so plainly laid out that no one can miss it. Whether you are a headhunter on a South Pacific island or an upscale yuppie in downtown Chicago—no one can miss the truth about God—and no one has ever missed it because God has made the truth about himself as plain as day. That's why Paul says in verse 20, "They are without excuse." The whole human race knows about God. No one can say, "I didn't know." That explains why every culture on earth has some conception of a Supreme Being, however flawed that conception might be. Man was made to look for answers outside of himself. He is incurably religious by nature. The French philosopher Pascal said that inside the heart of every man there is a "God-shaped vacuum." And Augustine said, "O Lord, you have made us for yourself. Our hearts are restless until they find rest in you." Ecclesiastes 3:11 says that God "has put "eternity into man's heart," meaning that the longing for ultimate answers comes from God himself. God put that longing inside the human heart to cause men to look up to him.

Atheism is the most unnatural philosophy on the face of the earth.

Idolatry is more natural than atheism because at least the idolater acknowledges a higher power outside of himself. For a man to be an atheist he must not only deny the truth about God that he sees in nature, he must also deliberately and repeatedly suppress the truth about God found in his own conscience. In the end it takes more faith *not* to believe in God. Several years ago Ray Comfort wrote a book with the clever title, *God Doesn't Believe in Atheists*. He's right. God exists whether you believe it or not. "The fool says in his heart, 'There is no God'" (Psalm 14:1). God loves atheists, just as he loves all the sinners of the world, and an atheist can be saved just like anyone else. Down deep the atheist knows there is a God—he just won't admit it.

A SAVING MANIFESTATION:
GOD REVEALED HIMSELF IN HIS SON,
THE LORD JESUS CHRIST

We are not left to ourselves to decide who God is. He reveals himself in nature, and he reveals himself in the human heart. But Christianity declares that God has supremely revealed himself in Jesus. If we want to know God, we must come on his terms—through his Son. Jesus said in John 14:6, "I am the way, and the truth, and the life. No one comes to the Father except through me." That verse isn't very popular today, but truth isn't determined by majority vote.

Credo

In this day of theological compromise and evangelical weakness, we must proclaim again the message that God's love is broad, reaching to the ends of the earth, so that anyone can be saved. But we must also declare that salvation comes *only* through Jesus Christ, and for those who will not come to God through Jesus, there is no other way.

PERSONAL TRANSFORMATION:
ONCE WE MEET GOD,
OUR LIVES ARE CHANGED FOREVER

"And without faith it is impossible to please him, for whoever would draw near to God must believe that he exists and that he rewards those who seek him" (Hebrews 11:6). There is a hunger for God in our day that is insatiable. That's why people read *The Da Vinci Code*, and that's why twelve million people have purchased Rick Warren's book *The Purpose-Driven Life*. Those two books could hardly be more opposite, but at the time of this writing both are on the *New York Times* best-seller list.

There is a hunger for God in our day that is insatiable.

My friends John and Anne Ockers served the Lord in Niger for many years. John told me how his first wife, Evelyn, died on the mission field and how he buried her in the missionary graveyard in Miango, Nigeria. When Marlene and I visited Nigeria a few years ago, we saw that missionary graveyard. It contains about sixty graves of men and women who made the ultimate sacrifice for the sake of the gospel. In the early part of the twentieth century the life expectancy of a missionary to Africa was only eight years. I saw a grave marker that read, "Placed in loving memory by his wife and children," then gave their names. Underneath were two words—"Abundantly Satisfied." So many markers. A child who died after one day. Another who lived a few days. A father and son buried side by side. He died trying to rescue his son from an overflowing creek. Both drowned.

Why would God permit such suffering for his servants who sacrificed so much for the gospel?

God's grace is free, but it is never cheap.

Reaching the world has never been easy, and Jesus knew that it wouldn't be. That's why he said, "In the world you will have tribulation" (John 16:33). Many centuries ago Tertullian declared that "the blood of the martyrs is the seed of the church." Wherever the church has gone, the cost of a new field has always been paid in blood. I saw a marker at Miango for a little child—a boy, I think—who died in the 1950s. The inscription read something like this: "We plant this seed in the hope that it will someday bear a harvest of souls for the Kingdom." When I walked back to my room, my eyes wet with tears, I said to Marlene, "When I think of how little I have placed on the altar . . ."

Our visit to the missionary graveyard took place a few years ago. Now let's run the clock forward to my recent visit with some retired missionaries in Florida. Day after day I listened to aged saints look back over a lifetime of service for Christ. I never heard the first word of regret by anyone for their decades of service in distant lands. Any of them could have had an easier life by staying at home, but they heard the call of God, and that settled the matter for them. Some of them endured many years of difficulties, and those who labored in Muslim lands often saw only a handful of converts at the end of it all. One woman said that at the end of her time in Africa, she knew of "three or perhaps four" Muslim converts. Back in the 1940s, when she was just starting out, she met an elderly SIM missionary who said, "Focus on the cross and not on the hardness of the Muslim religion." That is what they did—and they built hospitals, clinics, schools, churches, and mission stations in very remote areas.

Not only did they have no regrets, but I noticed a very definite gladness of heart. They truly knew how to "Serve the LORD with gladness! Come into his presence with singing!" (Psalm 100:2). That's the other side of it—visible joy, deep satisfaction with how things turned out.

Credo

It is bracing and good for the soul to be around saints of God who have no regrets and who display gladness of heart.

Those missionaries have known their share of hardship, discouragement, opposition, sickness, loss, frustration, loneliness, physical suffering, and spiritual warfare. But they do not dwell on these matters. They speak with excitement about seeing God at work changing hearts, lives, families, villages, and whole tribes by the power of the gospel. They have "count[ed] it all joy" (James 1:2) for the sake of serving Christ. It is inspiring and humbling to be around such great saints of God. The world barely knows they are here, but in heaven their names are written in gold.

They have proved that God truly rewards those who earnestly seek him.

There is no other reason to leave the comfort of home for decades of difficulty in distant lands. Because they believe that "God is," they heard his call and responded with willing hearts. They sought him, they found him, and now at the end of their pilgrimage they have no regrets but instead gladness of heart and a burning zeal to see the world come to Christ.

The Creed begins with the words "I believe in God" for a good reason. It's the biggest risk you'll ever take. It's not an easy road, but there is gladness along the way and joy at the end of the journey. Start seeking God with all your heart, and your life will never be the same.

THINK ABOUT IT!

1. Does everyone really know there is a God? How? Then why are some people atheists?

2. Do you agree that Jesus, the Son of God on earth as a man, was the supreme manifestation of God and his love for us? Why or why not?

3. Would you want "Abundantly Satisfied" on your tombstone? Why or why not? Are you satisfied and content in your life now? If not, how can you become so?

3

Who's in Charge Here?
"God, the Father Almighty"

He gives power to the faint, and to him who has no might he increases strength. Even youths shall faint and be weary, and young men shall fall exhausted; but they who wait for the LORD shall renew their strength.

ISAIAH 40:29-31

Define God in two words.

That's not easy to do, is it? But would we do better if we had twenty words, or a thousand words, or a million words? So let's take the assignment and look at it for a moment. Suppose you were asked to define God in only two words. Which words would you choose? It's a fascinating question because the Apostles' Creed compresses the entire nature of God into just two words—"Father Almighty." Interestingly, the phrase "Father Almighty" combines two words that don't normally go together. One of the common Greek words for Father is *Abba*, a very intimate term that means something like "Dear father" or "Papa." We might use the word "Daddy" today. The word "Almighty" in the Old Testament translates the Hebrew word *shaddai*, as in *El Shaddai*, "Almighty God." That name for God first appears in Genesis 17 when God informs Abram (who is ninety-nine years old) that a year later his wife Sarai (her name was later changed to Sarah) will give birth to a son. The very thought seems so absurd that Abram (whose name God changed to Abraham—"Father of Many Nations") laughed out loud. The Lord guaranteed the promise with his name—*El Shaddai*, the Lord Almighty. If we go all the way to the last book of the Bible, we find the name "Almighty" appearing several times. Revelation 1:8 is a typical example: "'I am the Alpha and the Omega,' says the Lord God, 'who is and who was and who is to come, the Almighty.'"

So the Apostles' Creed puts together two words that summarize who God is—one is intimate and personal, the other speaks of his unlimited power. To call him "Father" means that he is a personal God who cares about me. To call him "Almighty" means that he is able to do whatever needs to be done.

> The Apostles' Creed puts together two words that summarize who God is—one is intimate and personal, the other speaks of his unlimited power.

THE MAN FROM MISSISSIPPI

As I pondered the phrase "Father Almighty, " a new thought came to me. My dad was a "father almighty" to me. His story starts a few miles outside of Oxford, Mississippi. As a boy growing up on the farm, he learned how to hunt and fish, and he knew all about planting cotton and taking care of horses and cattle. During the Depression years when things were tough, he learned the value of hard work and the importance of saving every penny. After high school, he went off to college and then to the first two years of medical school. World War II intervened, and he became an Army doctor serving in Nome, Alaska. That's where he met my mother, an Army nurse. After the war they got married and moved to Memphis, where my older brother Andy and I were born. Later he moved to Russellville, Alabama, to take up the medical practice started by his brother Clarence, my namesake, who died in 1954 of a brain hemorrhage. That's why I grew up in a small town in Alabama. And that's where my dad lived until he died in 1974. We buried him on a hillside not far from his brother.

My dad always wore a coat and tie, treated people with respect, believed in good manners, and didn't think children should talk back to their parents. On that point my father might be called old-fashioned. He was old-school in another way too. Fathers today often try to be buddies to their children. My dad would have been mystified by that approach. Parents are parents, kids are kids, and the world works best when we all remember where we belong. Dad was not my best friend— he was my father. And there is a huge difference.

My father and I had a difficult relationship during my teenage years. He didn't understand me very well, and I didn't appreciate him as I should have. We had tense words on more than one occasion. The strain lasted into my college years when I began feeling the call into the ministry. I was young, immature, a little cocky, and I didn't know nearly as much as I thought I did. When I spoke of being a preacher, my dad made funny remarks that didn't seem funny to me. But looking back, I see that he knew me better than I knew myself. With the wisdom that only a father can have, he saw that I lacked the character necessary to be a pastor or a preacher. He knew that unless my life changed, I would not succeed.

In 1972 I attended a seminar where I heard for the first time about the importance of a clean conscience. The speaker said we couldn't be free to move forward until we asked forgiveness from those we had hurt. I knew I had to go talk to my dad. That wasn't an easy thing to do, but one night he was in his study at home, and I came in to see him. He was sitting at his desk catching up on some paperwork for the hospital, but he stopped what he was doing. I stammered out that I knew I had made a lot of mistakes and that I had hurt him and Mom by some of the things I had done, and I wanted him to know I was sorry for everything. He looked at me for a moment and then said, "That's all right, son." He didn't say anything else, but he didn't have to. I knew that I was forgiven.

JOSHUA TYRUS PRITCHARD

The next year Marlene and I got engaged, we graduated from college, and in June I told my parents in Alabama that we wanted to get married in Phoenix in August—six weeks later. Mom gasped. Dad smiled. He was the best man at my wedding. Dad died a little over two months after we were married. He was really healthy, then he was sick for two weeks, and then he was gone. One moment remains in my mind. After the funeral, Marlene and I were driving from Alabama back to Dallas where I was a first-year seminary student. Somewhere just across the Mississippi border I began to cry. I told Marlene a secret I had never shared with anyone. For a long time I had dreamed of having a son and naming him after my father. I wept because my father did not live to see it happen. Five years later our first son was born. We named him Joshua Tyrus, after my father, Tyrus Pritchard.

After my father died, it took me a while to see him properly. He had always been there whenever I needed him. He could answer any question. He could solve any problem. After he died, the world stopped being a safe place for me—and it's never seemed really safe again. I loved him, and I respected him, and I feared him, and I wanted him to be pleased with me. I still miss him. He was a "father almighty" to me.

STANDING IN THE PLACE OF GOD

It might seem like I have taken too much time in this chapter to talk about my father, but I think I am on good biblical footing. For a long time we have known that parents stand in the place of God for their children. Parents are not God, but we learn something about God (for better or for worse) from them. When the disciples asked Jesus to teach them to pray, he told them to start their prayers this way, "Our Father in heaven." Jesus himself compared earthly fathers with our Heavenly Father. "Or which one of you, if his son asks him for bread, will give him a stone? Or if he asks for a fish, will give him a serpent? If you then, who are evil, know how to give good gifts to your children, how much more will your Father who is in heaven give good things to those who ask him!" (Matthew 7:9-11). It is a father's joy and duty and honor to give his children what they truly need. My father did that for me, and I try to do that for my children. But I am a sinner, and my father was a sinner. There is only one perfect Father—our Father in heaven. He will do all that an earthly father will do and much more besides.

The circumstances surrounding our lives are no accident: they may be the work of evil, but that evil is held firmly within the mighty hand of our sovereign God. . . . All evil is subject to Him, and evil cannot touch His children unless He permits it. (Margaret Clarkson, GRACE GROWS BEST IN WINTER)

In Malachi 1:6 God declares, "A son honors his father, and a servant his master. If then I am a father, where is my honor? And if I am a master, where is my fear? says the LORD of hosts." This is one of the few places in the Bible where you find God as Father and God as Almighty in the same verse. If we believe in God as "the Father Almighty," then we owe him respect and honor.

Let me put these two concepts together so we can see them clearly:

- He is Almighty: He can do anything he wants to do. He is our Father: He will do all that is necessary for our well-being.
- He is Almighty: He can! He is our Father: He will!

To call him the Father Almighty means that we can trust him in every circumstance because he will do whatever needs to be done to take care of us.

To call him the Father Almighty means that we can trust him in every circumstance because he will do whatever needs to be done to take care of us. Romans 8:31-32 expresses this truth beautifully: "What then shall we say to these things? If God is for us, who can be against us? He who did not spare his own Son but gave him up for us all, how will he not also with him graciously give us all things?"

Whatever we truly need, our Father will make sure that we have it because he is the "Father Almighty"—El Shaddai—Almighty God.

39

Credo

Isaiah 40's promise of strength for the weary is based squarely on who God is:

> Have you not known? Have you not heard? The LORD is the everlasting God, the Creator of the ends of the earth. He does not faint or grow weary; his understanding is unsearchable. He gives power to the faint, and to him who has no might he increases strength. Even youths shall faint and be weary, and young men shall fall exhausted; but they who wait for the LORD shall renew their strength; they shall mount up with wings like eagles; they shall run and not be weary; they shall walk and not faint. (vv. 28-31)

The Father Almighty—that's the God I believe in.

"I WIN NO MATTER WHAT!"

When you know the Father Almighty, you have strength and courage to face the worst that life can throw your way. I received an e-mail from a man in Pennsylvania whose faith in God sustains him in the midst of an enormous personal crisis:

> As I write this I am suffering from Stage 4 Liver Cancer. I found out 3 weeks ago and at the present it is inoperable. I start chemo next week. I am 45 years old and it comes at the best time in our lives. We have 5 children and 3 grandchildren, everything was perfect till this. Don't get me wrong. I am not feeling sorry for myself, just the opposite. I believe that it had to be the worst so that the miracle will be the greatest. I win no matter what! Without chemo they say I have 6 months, with chemo, 2 years. The Love of Family and friends is overwhelming, I am being prayed for all over the U.S. as we speak. . . . God is in control, God is in charge of how everything turns out, God makes no mistakes, and God has our best interest at heart. I know cause He told me so.

That's a remarkable note in many ways. I love the sentence, "I win no matter what!" Only a man who believes in the Father Almighty can talk like that.

"If I truly believed in God the Father Almighty, I would _____." How would you fill in that blank? I hope I would trust him more and complain less. I would smile more and frown less. I would stop trying to play God, and I would let God be God in my life. I would be quicker to forgive and slower to get angry. I would risk more because I am secure in his love. I would be quicker to share Christ and less worried about what others think of me. I would say, "Your will be done," and I would mean it because my Father is not my enemy. I would pray more and pout less. I would enjoy what I already have, knowing that if I truly need something else, my Father in heaven will give it to me.

"God, the Father Almighty"—put your trust in him!

THINK ABOUT IT!

1. What did you learn about God from your father (or mother), positively or negatively? What effect is that having on your life right now?

2. Do you believe you will win regardless of how your trials turn out? Why or why not? What role does your faith in Christ play in this?

3. Do you need a greater understanding or appreciation of God either as a caring Father or as Almighty God? Why? What can you do to grow in this area?

4

Not by Chance:
"The Creator of Heaven and Earth"

"Worthy are you, our Lord and God, to receive glory and honor and power, for you created all things, and by your will they existed and were created."

REVELATION 4:11

Not long ago the Georgia state school superintendent proposed taking the word *evolution* out of the biology curriculum. Schools would still be required to teach evolution; they just wouldn't use the word. Former President Jimmy Carter said he was embarrassed by the proposal, which he called an attempt to censor and distort the education of Georgia students: "Nationwide ridicule of Georgia's public school system will be inevitable if this proposal is adopted, and additional and undeserved discredit will be brought on our excellent universities as our state's reputation is damaged."[8]

Please note the important point: This is not a dispute about evolution per se; it's only about the word *evolution*. The powers-that-be are so frightened by any challenge to the status quo that not only must evolution be taught—the word itself must be used.

In a related story, *World Magazine* named Phillip E. Johnson, law professor at the University of California, as its 2003 "Daniel of the Year" for his efforts to dismantle the Darwinist empire that dominates

American culture. In 1991 he sparked enormous controversy by publishing *Darwin on Trial* (Regnery, 1991; InterVarsity Press, 1993). In the years since then he has continued his attack on Darwinism through a steady stream of articles, books, speeches, debates, and other public appearances. He notes that many Christian leaders think the creation-evolution debate doesn't really matter. But they are terribly misguided. "The fundamental question is whether God is real or imaginary. The entire way of thinking that underlies Darwinian evolution assumes that God is out of the picture." He goes on to say that his greatest frustration comes not from dealing with the secular scientists (who are mostly, but not entirely, hostile to his arguments), but from Christian leaders who believe that evolution and the Christian faith are ultimately compatible.

> The more frustrating thing I think has been the Christian leaders and pastors, even very good pastors, especially Christian college and seminary professors. And there the problem is not just convincing them that the theory is wrong, but that it makes a difference. What's at stake isn't just the first chapter of Genesis, but the whole Bible from beginning to end.[9]

Professor Johnson is right on all points. What should we learn from this ongoing controversy?

THIS IS A CLASH OF COMPETING WORLDVIEWS

The debate about evolution and creation isn't really about the observable facts of science. And it's not about dinosaurs and DNA. It is really a debate between competing worldviews. Evolution at its heart views the world through a lens that is entirely naturalistic: It proposes to explain the entire universe without reference to God. As Johnson says, the evolutionist assumes that God either doesn't exist or doesn't matter. That means that this controversy is more important than finding the precise location of Noah's Ark or explaining the fossil layers in the Grand Canyon.

Evolution at its heart views the world through a lens that is entirely naturalistic: It proposes to explain the entire universe without reference to God.

The scientific issues serve as a kind of stalking-horse for the real metaphysical issues of ultimate truth. That's not a small thing since in evolutionary thinking there is no such thing as ultimate truth—only an endless series of theories first believed, then doubted, then discarded. Theologian Al Mohler offers this explanation:

> For over a hundred years, the dominant scientific establishment has been moving toward an enforced orthodoxy of naturalism, materialism, and secularism. According to this worldview, the universe is a closed box that can be understood only on its own terms—with everything inside the box explained only by other matter and processes within the same box. The box itself is explained as a cosmic accident, and naturalistic science allows no place for a designer or a design in the entire cosmos.[10]

That's why compromise positions such as theistic evolution never work. They attempt to join two things—creation and evolution—that are fundamentally incompatible. I realize many Christians—including some who hold to a high view of Scripture—believe in evolution as the best explanation of the origin of the human race. By so doing, they undermine the authority of the Bible by accommodating a contrary worldview.

THE CHRISTIAN WORLDVIEW RESTS UPON THE TRUTH THAT GOD CREATED ALL THINGS

"We created god in our own image and likeness!" So said comedian George Carlin, and he's right but not in the way he meant it. We didn't "create" God, but we did "create" a false god just like us, and that's the basic problem of the human race. It's also why the Creed puts the doctrine of creation in the second line. The Christian worldview stands

180 degrees removed from the evolutionary worldview. The biblical writers repeatedly ascribed all of creation to the work of God:

In the beginning, God created the heavens and the earth. (Genesis 1:1)

By faith we understand that the universe was created by the word of God, so that what is seen was not made out of things that are visible. (Hebrews 11:3)

Genesis 1 tells us something important about how God created. Eight times Genesis 1 repeats the phrase "And God said." He spoke, and light shined through the darkness. He spoke, and the waters receded from the earth. He spoke, and dry land appeared. He spoke, and vegetation appeared. He spoke, and the sun filled the sky by day and millions of stars twinkled by night. He spoke, and the sea teemed with fish and birds began to fly. He spoke, and cattle grazed, squirrels gathered hickory nuts, otters frolicked in the streams, and the kangaroo began hopping across the outback. Finally, he spoke again and created Adam. He breathed into him the breath of life, and Adam became a living soul. When Adam got lonely, God took a rib from his side and created Eve. Thus the human race began.

Perhaps you've seen those T-shirts that say, "I believe in the Big Bang. God said it . . . and BANG, it happened!" The Bible tells us plainly that the universe came into existence by God's command.

By the word of the LORD *the heavens were made; and all the host of them* by the breath of his mouth. *(Psalm 33:6, KJV)*

For he spake, and it was done; he commanded, and it stood fast. (Psalm 33:9, KJV)

For he commanded *and they were created. (Psalm 148:5, KJV)*

By the word of God the heavens were of old, and the earth standing out of water and in the water. (2 Peter 3:5, KJV)

In Revelation 4:11 we see the twenty-four elders (representing the redeemed of all the ages) cast their crowns before the throne of God in heaven and worship him: "Worthy are you, our Lord and God, to receive glory and honor and power, for you created all things, and by your will they existed and were created." A few verses later in Revelation 5, we see these same elders fall down and worship the Lamb, the Lord Jesus Christ, for the redemption he has purchased with his own blood: "Worthy are you to take the scroll and to open its seals, for you were slain, and by your blood you ransomed people for God from every tribe and language and people and nation" (v. 9).

Note that creation comes first, then redemption. The twenty-four elders first worship God because he is the Creator. Then they worship Christ because he is the Redeemer.

If we lose the doctrine of creation, we will eventually lose the doctrine of redemption.

Many evangelicals seem to have missed this fact. The story of creation leads to the reality of the fall. Genesis 1—2 tells us where we came from. Genesis 3 explains how sin entered the human race and why we need a Savior. Take away the factual reality of the first three chapters of the Bible and the rest cannot be trusted. That's what Phillip Johnson meant when he said what is at stake is not just the first chapters of Genesis, but every word of the Bible. Without creation there would be no redemption, no Christ dying on the cross, no forgiveness for our sins, no heaven, and no hope of eternal life.

If we see the majesty of God, we are able to see ourselves as we truly are. Human beings who respect God the Creator can begin to understand the mystery of their own being. (R. Kent Hughes, ROMANS)

But we should notice something else from Revelation 4:11. *God created all things by his own will.* The King James Version says he did it for his own pleasure. He created the universe because he wanted to, not because he needed to. Sometimes it is said that God created us because he was lonely in heaven, because he lacked something in himself.

That's a sentimental notion that has no basis in fact. We worship a God who exists eternally as Father, Son, and Holy Spirit—one God, three Persons. The Father, the Son, and the Holy Spirit love each other and fellowship together. God created us by an act of his own will. This is a high view of God's sovereignty, and it puts us in our proper position—facedown in the dust, humbled before our mighty Creator.

YOU WILL NEVER PROPERLY UNDERSTAND THE UNIVERSE UNTIL YOU KNOW THE GOD WHO CREATED IT

If you leave God out, you miss the fundamental truth about the universe! In order to understand human origins and the true history of the universe, we must begin not with the vain speculations of science, but with God's understanding as he has revealed it to us in his Word. Start there and you start on firm ground. Start anywhere else and you sink into the quicksand of humanistic unbelief.

We have to start with God. That's why the Apostles' Creed begins with the phrase, "I believe in God, the Father Almighty, the Creator of heaven and earth." When we put God at the center of all things, everything else finds its proper place. "The fear of the LORD is the beginning of wisdom, and the knowledge of the Holy One is insight" (Proverbs 9:10).

No one can know the universe and the answers to the great questions of life without knowing God.

The three great questions of life are:
• Where did I come from?
• Why am I here?
• Where am I going?

Until you answer the first question, you cannot answer the last two properly. If you think you evolved up from the slime, if you believe you arrived on the earth by chance as the result of blind evolution over millions or even billions of years, if you believe you are the product of an evolutionary stream that was started when a bolt of lightning hit primordial soup in the dim reaches of the distant past, then truly you don't know where you came from or why you are here or where you are going.

Three words summarize the biblical teaching regarding where we come from: *created, not evolved.* Teach that simple statement to your children. Make sure they know what it means. Let them learn that they were created by a personal God and that they did not evolve from some lower life-form. Then when they are older and are exposed to evolutionary ideas in the school system, tell them to give the required answers on the biology test but write at the bottom of the paper, "created, not evolved." It is imperative that our young people be fortified with the majestic biblical truth that they were created by God and are not the products of blind evolution. In his first public address, Pope Benedict XVI addressed this very issue: "We are not some casual and meaningless product of evolution. Each of us is the result of a thought of God. Each of us is willed, each of us is loved, each of us is necessary."[11]

It is imperative that our young people be fortified with the majestic biblical truth that they were created by God and are not the products of blind evolution.

When God put the world together, he put me in it just the way I am (apart from my sinfulness). He fashioned my arms, molded my bones, and knitted me together in my mother's womb. He made me nearsighted, left-handed, long-legged, with blue eyes, brown hair, illegible handwriting, and a Southern accent. He put inside me a passionate love for pepperoni pizza, chocolate pie, and chicken-fried steak. He called me to preach, gave me a love for writing, and blessed me beyond anything I deserve with a wonderful wife and three fine sons. I take two showers a day, I don't care for Brussels sprouts, I'm an Internet junkie, I ride my bike almost every day, and what they say is true—I can't jump. I don't dance very well, and I'm not much of a

Credo

singer. In short, God made me just the way I am. I'm a designer original, a limited edition of one, as unique as any snowflake that ever fell to the earth.

You too are a designer original. When God made you, he broke the mold. Because God made you, you belong here. It doesn't matter if you were a surprise to your parents. You weren't a surprise to God. We belong to God, he made us the way we are, and we couldn't escape him even if we tried. And we won't be happy until we know him intimately. He put a God-shaped vacuum inside your heart that only he can fill. He made you, he loves you in spite of your sin, and he sent his Son to die on the cross and rise from the dead so you could go to heaven. Your Creator has become your Savior. That's how much God loves you.

Everything starts with the God who created us. Start anywhere else and you will be perpetually confused. You'll never know who you are until you know who he is. That's why the Creed calls him "God, the Father Almighty, the Creator of heaven and earth."

THINK ABOUT IT!

1. What is your take on the creation-evolution debate as a clash of worldviews? On which side do you stand? Why?

2. What does God's being the Creator of the whole universe (including you!) mean to you personally? What impact does it have on your daily life? Do you agree that you can't understand the cosmos without a growing personal relationship with God?

3. Do you really believe that you are a designer original, a special creation of an all-powerful, loving God? Why or why not? Do you feel like a special creation? If not, what can you do to make this truth more real in your life?

5

The Incomparable Christ: "Jesus Christ, His Only Son, Our Lord"

God is faithful, by whom you were called into the fellowship of his Son, Jesus Christ our Lord.

1 CORINTHIANS 1:9

Who is Jesus Christ? It is no exaggeration to say that this is the central question of history and the most important issue anyone will ever face. Who is he? Where did he come from? Why did he come? What difference does his coming make in my life? In the end, every person must deal with Jesus Christ. You can avoid the question, or postpone it, or pretend you didn't hear it. But sooner or later you must answer it.

It's certainly not a new question. It's as old as the coming of Christ to earth. Once when Jesus took his disciples on a retreat to a place called Caesarea Philippi, he asked them, "Who do people say that the Son of Man [referring to himself] is?" They offered four responses: John the Baptist, Elijah, Jeremiah, or one of the prophets (see Matthew 16:13-16). Even when he walked on this earth, people were confused as to his true identity.

The discussion has continued across the centuries, to this very day. Here are some contemporary views: A good man. The Son of God. A

51

prophet. A Galilean rabbi. A teacher of God's Law. The embodiment of God's love. A reincarnated spirit master. The ultimate revolutionary. The Messiah of Israel. The Savior. A first-century wise man. A man just like any other man. King of kings. A misunderstood teacher. Lord of the Universe. A deluded religious leader. Son of Man. A fabrication of the early church.

Today people give all of those possible answers. Two thousand years have passed, and still we wonder about the man called Jesus. That takes us back to Caesarea Philippi. After Jesus asked for the opinions of others, he turned to his closest supporters and asked for their answer: "But who do you say that I am?" In the end, each of us faces the same question. We can't get away with quoting the opinions of others. We each have to make up our own mind.

Who is Jesus Christ? And how does your answer stack up with the Bible? That's an important second question because it is not enough to say, "I believe in Jesus." Millions of people claim to believe in him but don't have a clue about what the Bible says about him. Which Jesus do you believe in?

IT'S ALL ABOUT JESUS

Thankfully, we don't have to wonder who Jesus is. For two thousand years Christians have affirmed their faith in Jesus with these words from the Apostles' Creed: "I believe in . . . Jesus Christ, [God's] only Son, our Lord." This phrase begins the second major section of the Creed. The Creed itself is Trinitarian—with a section devoted to the Father, a section to the Son, and a final section to the Holy Spirit. Of the 110 words in the Creed, seventy occur in the section relating to Jesus Christ. That tells us something important.

The Christian faith is all about Jesus!

He is the heart and core of all that we believe. You can be mistaken on some secondary issues and still be a Christian, but being wrong about Jesus is deadly. Our faith in Jesus must be more than just an emotional experience of "having Jesus in my heart." Our faith must rest on the revealed truth about Jesus Christ, God's only Son, our Lord.

If we take this clause from the Creed and examine it, we can see that it contains four statements:

- I believe in Jesus.
- I believe he is the Christ.
- I believe he is God's only Son.
- I believe he is the Lord.

Each of these statements deserves close examination. J. I. Packer notes that when the Creed calls God "the Creator of heaven and earth," it parts company with Hinduism and by extension all Eastern religions. And when it declares that Jesus is the Christ, God's only Son, and our Lord, it parts company with Islam and Judaism. This claim for Jesus makes Christianity utterly unique.[12]

These titles were commonly used by early Christians to describe their faith. Sometimes they used the familiar symbol of the fish, which in Greek is *IXTHUS*, and was used as an acrostic for four words found in this phrase of the Creed and one that is not:

The letter *I* is the first letter of *Jesus* in Greek.
The letter *X* is the first letter of *Christ* in Greek.
The letters *TH* stand for the first letter of *God* in Greek.
The letter *U* is the first letter of *Son* in Greek.
The letter *S* is the first letter of *Savior* in Greek.

So the word *IXTHUS* (and the fish symbol) stood as shorthand for:

Jesus Christ, God's Son, our Savior.

HE IS THE SAVIOR

The name *Jesus* means "God saves." Scholars tell us that it was actually a very common name among the Jews in the first century. At least ten other men named Jesus lived in Judea at the same time as our Lord. At least five Jewish high priests were named Jesus. The name itself is the Greek version of the Old Testament name Joshua. It speaks of the fact that God has entered the human race on a rescue mission from heaven. That's why the angel said to Joseph, "You shall call his name Jesus, for he will save his people from their sins" (Matthew 1:21).

When we say we believe in Jesus, we mean that he was fully human and yet fully divine—a man like us, yet a man who possessed the very attributes of God himself.

The God-man came to save us from our sins.

HE IS THE CHRIST

Despite what some might think, Christ is not Jesus' last name. It's a title. To be precise, we should call him Jesus the Christ. When you see President Bush on TV, you know that President is not his first name; it's his title, the name of the office he holds. In the same way, the term *Christ* describes one of the Son's divinely-appointed titles. It comes from a Greek word that itself comes from a Hebrew word that means "the anointed one." We often translate it as "the Messiah." In the Old Testament, prophets, priests, and kings were anointed when they formally began their service for God. The anointing was a sign that God had called them to their position. To call Jesus "the Christ" means that he is the one whom God had promised to send to deliver Israel and to bring salvation to the world.

> To call Jesus "the Christ" means that he is the one whom God promised to send to deliver Israel and to bring salvation to the world.

A river of connected history flows from Genesis to Revelation, spanning thousands of years and hundreds of generations. Although the Bible contains sixty-six books written by many different people over fifteen hundred years, it has one message: *God's plan to bring salvation to the world through Jesus Christ.* Everything in the Bible fits around that great theme.

Old Testament—anticipation
Gospels—incarnation
Acts—proclamation
Epistles—explanation
Revelation—consummation

The Old Testament says, "He is coming!" The Gospels say, "He is here!" The book of Acts says, "He has come!" The Epistles say, "He is Lord!" Revelation says, "He is coming again!"

The Old Testament contains many promises of his coming:

- He will be the seed or offspring of the woman (Genesis 3:15).
- He will be a descendant of Shem (Genesis 9:26; 11:10-32).
- He will be a descendant of Abraham (Genesis 12:2-3).
- He will come from the tribe of Judah (Genesis 49:10).
- He will be a descendant of David (2 Samuel 7:11-16).
- He will be born of a virgin (Isaiah 7:14).
- He will be born in Bethlehem (Micah 5:2).

Only one person in history fits them all those qualifications: Jesus Christ. So we say to our Jewish friends, with love and respect, "The One for whom you are waiting has already come to earth. He came two thousand years ago. He is your Messiah. His name is Jesus Christ."

To say that Jesus is the Christ means that he is the One sent from God to bring God to us and to bring us to God.

HE IS GOD'S ONLY SON

The little word *only* tells us something crucial about our Lord. In the King James translation of John 3:16, we are told that God so loved the world that he sent his "only begotten" Son. That phrase comes from the Greek word *monogenas*. The *mono* part means "one" or "only," as in the word *monologue*, one person speaking to many people. The *genas* part is related to the English words *gene*, *genetics*, and *gender*. When both parts are put together, "only begotten" means "one and only" or "unique." Jesus Christ is one of a kind.

> A man who is merely a man and said the things that Jesus said wouldn't be a great moral teacher; he'd either be a lunatic on a level with the man who says he's a poached egg or else a devil of hell—an evil liar. You must make your choice; either this man was and is the Son of God or else a madman or something worse. But don't let us come up with any of this patronizing nonsense about him being a great human teacher; he hasn't left that open to us. He didn't intend to. . . . Now it seems to me obvious, that he was neither a lunatic nor fiend and consequently, no matter how strange, frightening or unlikely it may seem, I have to accept the view that he was and is God. (C. S. Lewis, MERE CHRISTIANITY)

Because the Son shares in the same nature as the Father, Jesus could say, "I and the Father are one" (John 10:30). His Jewish hearers understood him to be claiming equality with God. To call Jesus God's only Son means that he shares the same essential nature as the Father.

From this truth comes the doctrine of the Trinity—one God eternally existing in three divine Persons—Father, Son, and Holy Spirit.

The Nicene Creed succinctly states that Jesus Christ is "very God of very God." To call him God's only Son means that he is God the Son and is thus worthy of the same worship, adoration, praise, and reverence that we give to God the Father.

HE IS OUR LORD

Jesus is "our Lord." The Greek word is *kurios*. This word occurs many times in the New Testament, and it was also common throughout the Roman Empire. Its basic meaning is "absolute ruler." To call Jesus *Lord* means that he is sovereign over the entire universe, and thus he has the right to rule you and me. Romans 10:9 says, "if you confess with your mouth that Jesus is Lord and believe in your heart that God raised him from the dead, you will be saved." Notice how simple that phrase is— "Jesus is Lord." To confess with the mouth means more than simply saying the words. It means to agree from the heart that you believe what you are saying.

To call Jesus *Lord* means that he is sovereign over the entire universe, and thus he has the right to rule you and me.

In order to understand this properly, we need a bit of background on how the Romans ruled their vast empire. Because the empire stretched from Europe into the Middle East and across the northern coast of Africa, it encompassed many provinces and included many local religions. "Mystery religions" were found in many parts of the empire. Each religion has its own code of conduct, sacred scriptures, pattern of worship, form of sacrifice, sacred rites, priesthood, and so on. Because these religions tended to keep people pacified, the Romans left them alone as much as possible. Rome required only that taxes be paid and that everyone be required to say, "Caesar is Lord." "Just affirm that Caesar is sovereign and follow whatever religion suits you."

For many people in the Empire, that was no big burden. But Christians couldn't say "Caesar is Lord" and remain faithful to Christ. How could they say, "Caesar is Lord" when their faith taught them that Jesus is Lord? They refused to deny Christ, and that is why Christians were murdered by the thousands—crucified, burned at the stake, run through with the sword, thrown to wild animals.

Chuck Colson notes that in the first century if you stood in a public gathering and cried out, "Jesus is God!" no one would be upset. But if you shouted, "Jesus is Lord!" you would start a riot. Rome did not persecute Christians because they believed in the deity of Christ or proclaimed that Jesus was the promised Messiah or that Jesus died on the cross and rose from the dead. Rome did not kill Christians because they said Jesus is the only way of salvation. Those religious beliefs did not threaten the state. But when Christians declared, "Jesus Christ is our Lord, and there is no other!" that was a direct attack on Caesar-worship and thus punishable by death.

To call him Lord means we surrender all we have to him and follow him gladly wherever he leads, whatever it costs.

THE NAME ABOVE EVERY NAME

Therefore God has highly exalted him and bestowed on him the name that is above every name, so that at the name of Jesus every knee should bow, in heaven and on earth and under the earth, and every tongue confess that Jesus Christ is Lord, to the glory of God the Father. (Philippians 2:9-11)

God has ordained that one day his Son will be universally recognized as the Lord of heaven and earth.

Many people didn't recognize him when he walked on the earth. Most people today still don't know who he is. But a day is coming when that will change forever. Then every knee will bow, and every tongue will confess that Jesus Christ is Lord. All creation will acknowledge his lordship. This includes all who are "in heaven and on earth and under the earth"—angels and saints in heaven; all those living on the earth and the dead; demons and Satan himself under the earth. Bowing with the knee, all will declare that Jesus Christ is Lord and will submit to him. They will confess that there is no Lord but Jesus.

Jesus will have the last word! He will be vindicated before the entire universe. Even his enemies will bow before him. In the end no opposition against him will stand. Not all will be saved, but all will confess that Jesus is Lord.

> **Jesus will have the last word! He will be vindicated before the entire universe. Even his enemies will bow before him.**

THE PASTORS' ROUNDTABLE

Several years ago I took part in a roundtable on a local Christian radio station. Since it happened on December 22, I thought we would have a nice, friendly talk about the meaning of Christmas. Wrong! There were three people on the panel—a Messianic Jewish Rabbi, me, and a Muslim cleric. Gone were my visions of eggnog and candy canes. We spent the first hour talking about politics and the situation in the Middle East in the light of 9/11. In the second hour the discussion turned to spiritual issues. The host wanted to know if Jews, Muslims, and Christians all worship the same God. The Messianic Jewish Rabbi and I both said no; the Muslim cleric said yes.

I countered by saying that Christians believe you cannot speak about God without speaking of his Son, the Lord Jesus Christ. We cannot say, "We have God with Jesus, and you have God without Jesus," as if Jesus is some kind of optional equipment, like a padded steering wheel—nice but not necessary.

Back and forth the discussion went. Eventually the Muslim cleric said that Muslims love Jesus too. They revere him as a prophet of God, and they even believe in his Virgin Birth and in his miracles. But they don't believe he is the Son of God because God cannot have a son. And they don't believe he died on the cross; they believe he only *appeared* to die. Therefore they don't believe in the resurrection. Nevertheless, they love Jesus too. Of course, those denied *details* (my word, not his) comprise the heart and soul of who Jesus really is. At that point the host turned to me and said, "Pastor Ray, I guess in the end it all comes down to Jesus, doesn't it? He's really the central issue. Do you agree with that?" I said that in the end, Jesus is indeed the central issue of the human race. Each of us will one day give an account for what we have done with the Lord Jesus Christ. Did we love him and serve him as Savior and Lord or reject him?

On the spur of the moment I began to paraphrase Philippians 2:9-11. "A day is coming when every knee will bow and every tongue will confess that Jesus Christ is Lord. That doesn't just include Christians—that includes everyone everywhere. We will all bow down and proclaim him as Lord to the glory of God the Father." I don't want to wait. I want to bow my knee right now and worship him as my Lord.

We must declare this, especially to those who don't want to hear it. Recently a friend told me about a family member who said in all seriousness, "If you ever mention Jesus to me, I will never speak to you again." When such moments come, we need to respond with words like these: "I don't want to lose your friendship, but I must tell you the truth. You were made by Jesus Christ. You owe your life to him. You can bow before him today as your Savior or you can face him one day as your Judge, but you cannot escape him. The choice is yours." Will you bow before him in love and adoration, or in abject terror moments before you are cast into eternal hell?

"I believe in . . . Jesus Christ, [God's] only Son, our Lord." This is the Jesus of the Bible. This is the Christ we worship. This is the Jesus we call Savior and Lord. This is the true Christ of the Christian faith. There is no one like him, for he alone is God incarnate. His words have divine authority because they are the words of Almighty God. One day the entire universe will bow down and worship him. We have no other Savior, and we follow no other Lord. The martyrs died because they would not worship anyone else. We will not exchange the Lord Jesus Christ for anyone or anything. God hasten the day when every knee shall bow and every tongue confess that Jesus Christ is Lord to the glory of God the Father!

THINK ABOUT IT!

1. Jesus Christ, God's Son, our Savior. Which of those titles for Jesus means the most to you? Why?

2. Is it more or less popular (or advantageous) to publicly call Jesus Lord now than it was in the days of the Roman Empire? In what ways? How can doing this make life difficult for you?

3. Do you regularly confess Jesus Christ as your Lord? How does your faith in him manifest itself in your life?

6

Why the Virgin Birth Matters: "Conceived of the Holy Spirit, Born of the Virgin Mary"

Behold, the virgin shall conceive and bear a son, and shall call his name Immanuel [God with us].

ISAIAH 7:14; MATTHEW 1:23

Let's begin our study with two familiar verses of Scripture:

> *But as he considered these things, behold, an angel of the Lord appeared to him in a dream, saying, "Joseph, son of David, do not fear to take Mary as your wife, for that which is conceived in her is from the Holy Spirit." (Matthew 1:20)*

> *The angel answered her, "The Holy Spirit will come upon you, and the power of the Most High will overshadow you; therefore the child to be born will be called holy—the Son of God." (Luke 1:35)*

The first verse tells us what the angel said to Joseph to reassure him about Mary's pregnancy. The second verse is part of what the angel Gabriel said to Mary when he announced that she would give birth to Jesus. Taken together, these verses form a fitting introduction to the next section of the Apostles' Creed: "I believe in . . . Jesus Christ . . . who was conceived of the Holy Spirit, born of the Virgin Mary." Here we come face to face with the Virgin Birth of Christ—a doctrine we tend not to think about except during December. But the early Christians esteemed this truth so highly that they included it in the first Christian creed. Therefore, it must be of paramount importance, a foundational doctrine of our faith. Here are three simple statements about the Virgin Birth of Christ:

It is clearly taught in the Bible. Isaiah prophesied it seven hundred years before Christ's birth. Matthew and Luke explicitly included it in their Gospels.

It has been universally believed. This doctrine reaches across the various divisions of Christendom—Orthodox, Catholic, Protestant, and Evangelical.

It has also been hotly debated. Until the last 150 years, few people challenged this teaching. With the rise of liberal Christianity, some theologians have dubbed this doctrine a fanciful superstition or have called it a legend created to make Jesus seem divine or have said the church borrowed a pagan myth or Jewish tradition or have declared that the silence of the New Testament outside of Matthew and Luke regarding the Virgin Birth must mean either that it doesn't matter or it didn't happen. If you go all the way back to the Gospel accounts, you can find hints here and there that even in Jesus' lifetime there were rumors about his unusual parentage. Some people thought he was the product of an act of immorality. A pagan opponent of the early church said that Jesus was the result of a sexual encounter between Mary and a Roman soldier. That slander and others similar to it (consider *The Da Vinci Code*) has been repeated across the generations down to the present day.

The Virgin Birth rests on the great divide that separates those who believe the Bible is God's Word and those who don't. It separates those who believe in a supernatural Christ from those who believe he was merely a good man, a moral teacher, a revolutionary, or a prophet.

Christians make a claim for Jesus that cannot be made for any other person: His life did not begin with his birth or with his conception.

Christians make a claim for Jesus that cannot be made for any other person: His life did not begin with his birth or with his conception. Unlike every other human whose beginning can be traced to a specific moment in time, the life of Jesus Christ had no beginning. Because he is eternal, he has always existed, along with God the Father and God the Holy Spirit. This is an utterly supernatural claim that could not be made about anyone else.

WHAT DOES THE VIRGIN BIRTH MEAN?

What exactly do we mean when we say that Jesus was "conceived of the Holy Spirit" and "born of the Virgin Mary"? First, *Jesus was born by the direct action of God.* Clearly no one was expecting anything like this. Joseph assumes the worst until the angel intervenes. Mary is shocked and mystified by Gabriel's words. The Jews in general had no conception of a baby being born to a virgin who would deliver them. God did it this way because he chose to do it this way. A virgin gave birth by the sovereign choice of Almighty God.

Second, *no man was involved in the process.* Not Joseph, not a Roman soldier, not any other man. Third, *Jesus had a human mother and no human father.* Fourth, *Jesus is thus fully human and fully divine.* He is fully human because he came forth from Mary's womb. He is fully divine because he was conceived by the Holy Spirit. He is not half-human and half-divine. He is the God-man—one person possessing two natures—God incarnate in human flesh. Fifth, *he is therefore without sin.* He has no inherited sin from Adam, nothing in him that will cause him to sin. He is holy in the truest and deepest meaning of that term—sinless.

In order for Christ to be our Savior, three conditions had to be met:
- *He must be a man.* An angel could not die for our sins.
- *He must be an infinite man.* A mere mortal could not bear the infinite price that had to be paid for our sins.
- *He must be an innocent man.* A sinner could not die for the sins of others.

Credo

The Virgin Birth guarantees that our Lord fulfills all three conditions.
Because he was born of Mary, he is fully human. Because he was
conceived by the Holy Spirit, he is fully God. Because he was born holy,
he is sinless in thought, word, and deed. Thus he is fully qualified to
be our Savior.

HOW DID THE VIRGIN BIRTH HAPPEN?

What exactly took place when the Holy Spirit conceived the human life
of Jesus within Mary's womb? How could the God who is without lim-
its somehow shrink himself, so to speak, inside Mary's womb? We don't
know because what happened was a miracle of the highest order, to be
compared with God's saying, "Let there be light" and light appearing
out of the darkness. The virginal conception of Jesus was a direct, creative miracle of God. It is also a mystery we will never fully understand.
In these days of amazing technological advancement, we occasionally
hear talk about science reproducing a "virgin birth" today. Despite the
accomplishments in genetic manipulation, cloning, parthenogenesis,
and other advanced research, all the scientists from the best labs, even
if they had unlimited resources and a thousand years, cannot duplicate
the virginal conception of Christ. Only God himself can create a life
that is fully human and yet fully divine. Jesus Christ is truly God's one
and only Son. This is a miracle and a mystery that lies beyond the reach
of science.

Whenever you are occupied in the matter of your salvation, set
aside all curious speculations about God's unsearchable majesty,
all thought of works, traditions, philosophy, and even God's law,
and run straight to the manger. Embrace this infant, the Virgin's
little baby, in your arms; see him as he was born, sucking, growing
up, living among people, teaching, dying, rising again, ascending
above all the heavens, and having power over all things. In this way
you will be able to shake off all terrors and errors, just as the sun
drives away the clouds. And contemplating this will keep you in the
right way, so that you can follow where Christ has gone. (Martin
Luther, GALATIANS)

Luke 1:35 offers a hint of what happened when the angel says that the power of the Most High will "overshadow" Mary. That same verb was used in the Greek translation of Exodus 40:35: "Moses was not able to enter the tent of meeting because the cloud settled on it, and the glory of the LORD *filled* the tabernacle." Psalm 91:4 uses the same word in a poetic image to describe God covering his people: "He will *cover* you with his pinions, and under his wings you will find refuge; his faithfulness is a shield and buckler." These images give us some idea of what happened. God "overshadowed" Mary with his personal, intimate presence that completely surrounded her just as the cloud surrounded, covered, and filled the tabernacle. And this overshadowing protected her from all harm. She was a virgin before her conception and after her conception. Only God could have done this.

Through the Virgin Birth, God became man without ceasing to be God.

When I preached this to my congregation, I took off my suit coat and laid it on the choir rail. I told the people that my white shirt represented the deity of Jesus Christ. Then I asked the congregation, "Do I have to wear my jacket in order to wear my shirt?" The obvious answer is no. I can wear my shirt with or without my coat. In the same way, Jesus was always the Son of God and always will be. When he was in the manger, he was the Son of God. When he walked on the Sea of Galilee, he was the Son of God. When he died on the cross, he was the Son of God. When he rose from the dead, he was the Son of God. When he went back to heaven, he was the Son of God. When he comes again, he will be the Son of God. Nothing can ever change his essential nature.

He was and is and always will be the Son of God.

Having said that, I then put my coat back on and told the congregation that it represented the human nature Christ took upon himself when he came to the earth. Then I asked, "Am I still wearing my white shirt?" I was. "This isn't a magic trick, and I'm not David Copperfield. But (and this is a crucial point) you can't see the white shirt very easily because it is mostly covered by my coat. It's still there—I never took it off—but when I wear my coat, it's easy to miss." This explains why many people didn't know who Jesus was. They saw him wearing his coat of humanity and assumed that was all there was. But as John 1:14 says, "The Word became flesh and dwelt among us." Christ, the living Word, put on humanity the same way I put on my coat before I go to church every Sunday morning. He was always God, but he "added" humanity through the Virgin Birth.

WHAT DIFFERENCE DOES THE VIRGIN BIRTH MAKE?

The major problem with a study like this may be that most of us already believe in the Virgin Birth. Even if we've never thought about it very much, we know we believe it because we hear about it every December. So it's easy to put this part of the Creed in the category of, "Nice, but so what?" That would be a huge mistake. We can be certain that the early Christians didn't feel that way or they wouldn't have included these phrases in the Creed. Jesus' being "conceived of the Holy Spirit" and "born of the Virgin Mary" has three important implications.

Biblical Authority

Since both Matthew and Luke explicitly teach the Virgin Birth, we are immediately faced with a major question: Will we accept what Scripture plainly teaches? For centuries few people asked that question, but starting 150 years ago it became a major issue. The problem for us can be stated this way: Matthew and Luke tell us that Jesus entered the world in a supernatural way—through a mighty miracle of God. These same writers tell us that Jesus' earthly life came to a climax with another mighty miracle—his bodily resurrection from the dead. Regarding the latter, we all understand the significance of the Resurrection: Because he lives, we too shall live. His resurrection guarantees ours. But it's not the same with the Virgin Birth. His supernatural birth doesn't tell us anything about our physical birth. And since we've already been born, it's easy to discount the Virgin Birth when we compare it to the Resurrection. But if you can't believe the first miracle, how can you believe the last miracle? If you doubt the Virgin Birth, how can you be certain about the Resurrection? The Bible doesn't present the life of Christ as a kind of "pick your miracle" cafeteria where you can pick one and reject another.

The story of our Lord's earthly life comes to us as a seamless whole. We either take it all or we reject it all.

There is no suitable middle-ground option. So the question becomes, do we believe the Bible or don't we? At this point I'm happy to give thanks for that famous "theologian" Mel Gibson. During a televised interview with Diane Sawyer, he was asked if he believes every word of the Bible is true. He answered with an immediate and unequivocal yes. Then he added, "Either you believe all of it or none of it." That's one reason the Virgin Birth matters. It's a question of biblical authority.

Jesus Christ

The Virgin Birth forces us to confront what we believe about Jesus Christ. Who is he? Where did he come from? At issue is the supernatural character of our Lord. Is he truly the Son of God from heaven? If you answer yes, you'll have no problem with the Virgin Birth. If you answer no, you'll have no reason to believe it. Is he just a prophet, or a great teacher, or a martyr, or a revolutionary who never intended to start a religion? Or is he God incarnate, the Lord of Glory, the Son of God, our Lord and our Savior? The Virgin Birth tells us that we can't be neutral and we can't say the stories of his birth don't matter. Those with an anti-supernatural bias will have no use for the Virgin Birth, and they will try to explain it away. But those who believe in a supernatural Christ will find the Virgin Birth a mysterious miracle that, instead of destroying their faith, actually makes it stronger.

Those who believe in a supernatural Christ will find the Virgin Birth a mysterious miracle that, instead of destroying their faith, actually makes it stronger.

In order for Jesus to be our Savior he had to be a man, God, and sinless. The Virgin Birth guarantees that all those conditions have been met.

Thus there is a direct connection between the manger and the cross.

Without his Virgin Birth, his sufferings have no meaning. His birth makes his death meaningful. His birth establishes his true identity as the Son of God, the promised Messiah, our Savior. When the angel told Joseph that the baby Mary was carrying had been conceived by the Holy Spirit, in the very next breath he told Joseph to name him Jesus, "for he will save his people from their sins" (Matthew 1:21). The angel connects his birth with his saving work on the cross. Thus the Virgin Birth matters greatly because it tells us plainly who Jesus is and lays the foundation for the great work he would accomplish on the cross.

Salvation

By means of the Virgin Birth, Christ becomes the beginning of a new humanity. Because he is born of Mary, he is truly human; because he is conceived of the Holy Spirit, he is free from the inherited guilt handed down from Adam. Thus he is fully able to stand in our place, taking our guilt, our shame, our punishment.

He could pay for our sins precisely because he had no sin and no guilt of his own.

He who knew no sin became sin for us so that we might receive the righteousness of God through him (2 Corinthians 5:21). This brings to the forefront Paul's words in Romans 5:6, "For while we were still weak, at the right time Christ died for the ungodly." Christ succeeded where Adam (and all of Adam's descendants) failed. We were so helpless that we could not do anything to save ourselves.

The Virgin Birth teaches us that our salvation is entirely supernatural.

When God wanted to save the world, he had to take the initiative. We were helpless even to take the first step in the process of bringing

Christ to the world. The Virgin Birth teaches us that salvation is entirely by grace. God does it all because we could not do any of it.[13]

The Virgin Birth reminds us that we all need a Savior.

Leif Jonasen

Today we may want a teacher or a leader or a pastor to guide us. But when we stand at death's door, only a Savior can lead us safely through to the other side. A few years ago Leif and Nancy Jonasen started attending the church I pastor, Calvary Memorial Church. Nancy served in the nursery, and Leif built sets for our church's Christmas programs. A couple of years ago Leif was diagnosed with leukemia. The doctors told him up front that the disease might eventually take his life. The first time I visited him in the hospital, we talked openly about the seriousness of his situation. He knew that he was fighting for his life. But he told me with a smile, "It's a win-win situation for me. If I am cured, I win. If I die, I win because I will go to be with Jesus."

Over the next few months he underwent grueling chemotherapy. Later he endured a very difficult stem-cell transplant. His hair fell out, he lost weight, and he felt awful for many weeks at a time. There were moments when the nausea and sickness seemed overwhelming. We didn't see him in church very often because of his treatments. But after the transplant the leukemia went into remission, his hair began to grow again, and he came to church with Nancy as often as possible. And there was always a smile.

One day the doctor called with bad news. A blood test showed that the leukemia had returned. This was a very heavy blow. Even though they always knew it was a possibility, they had hoped and prayed it would not happen. On top of the leukemia, Leif developed a severe case of pneumonia. His condition deteriorated over the next twenty-four hours; so the doctors put him on a ventilator. Nancy e-mailed me that his situation had become extremely critical. When my wife, Marlene, and I arrived at his room in the ICU, we found that he had been heavily sedated so they could treat him more easily. After talking with Nancy for a few minutes, I took a Bible and stood next to Leif and began to talk to him as if he were wide-awake. I did that because I don't believe that any medicine or any sickness can prevent the Lord's Word from getting through to the Lord's people.

"Leif, this is Pastor Ray. I want to read some Scripture to you." So I read Psalm 23: "The Lord is my shepherd; I shall not want." And John 14: "In my Father's house are many rooms." And 2 Corinthians 5: "away from the body and at home with the Lord." And Philippians 1: "To me to live is Christ, and to die is gain." Finally I read those wonderful verses from 1 Thessalonians 4: "The dead in Christ will rise first." When I was finished, I prayed for Leif. My final words to him were, "We will see you again."

Later Nancy called with the news that he was down to his final few hours. On Saturday morning Marlene and I arrived at the hospital about 10 A.M. The family had gathered around Leif's bed. They had been singing some of his favorite hymns. It was obvious that he had only a short time left. I read the last few verses of 1 Corinthians 15: "O death, where is your victory? O death, where is your sting?"

Members of the family took turns saying good-bye. Every so often Nancy leaned down to whisper something to her beloved husband. A few minutes later they began to sing, "Amazing grace—how sweet the sound—that saved a wretch like me! I once was lost, but now am found, was blind, but now I see." Then the last verse: "When we've been there ten thousand years, bright shining as the sun, we've no less days to sing God's praise than when we've first begun."

A few minutes later he breathed his last. A nurse came in and said, "He has passed." I thought to myself, *She said more than she knew.* Leif Jonasen passed from death to life, from suffering and pain to a life of eternal joy, from the valley of the shadow of death into the personal presence of Jesus Christ. He passed from this dark world into the light of eternal day.

We all need a Savior sooner or later. When you face death, you don't need a teacher—you need Jesus. When you have to cross the river of no return, a myth won't help you—you need a Savior. And we have one. His name is Jesus Christ.

THINK ABOUT IT!

1. Do you find it easy or difficult to believe that Jesus was truly born of a virgin, a supernatural birth? Why?

2. Do you think it really matters whether or not a person accepts the Virgin Birth as literally true? Why? What does doubt or denial about it do to one's faith or spiritual commitment?

3. When the time of your own departure from this world comes, will you be able to face it confidently? On whom will you most depend to see you through that ordeal—a pastor, a teacher, a family member, a friend, your own faith, or a personal Savior? Explain.

7

The Man Who Killed Jesus:
"Suffered Under Pontius Pilate"

He was wounded for our transgressions; he was crushed for our iniquities; upon him was the chastisement that brought us peace, and with his stripes we are healed. All we like sheep have gone astray; we have turned every one to his own way; and the LORD has laid on him the iniquity of us all.

ISAIAH 53:5-6

Mel Gibson did something Billy Graham could not do. For a few weeks in the late winter and early spring of 2004, he brought Jesus into the center of American public life. Consider what happened on the day *The Passion of the Christ* premiered in theaters around the country. That morning I turned on the news to see what was happening in the world. On CBS they were talking about Jesus. On NBC they were talking about Jesus. On ABC they were talking about Jesus. On Fox News Channel they were talking about Jesus. On CNN they were talking about Jesus. That afternoon I saw the film with a friend. When I got home, I turned on the TV and happened to watch CNBC, the cable channel that specializes in financial news. But they weren't talking about stocks and bonds. That afternoon they were talking about Jesus. In fact, they were talking about why Jesus died on the cross.

A few nights later 450 people from the church I pastor attended a showing of *The Passion of the Christ* at a local theater. Afterward we came back to the church for a meal and a time of discussion. Between the film and the meal, I went home for a few minutes. When I turned on the Fox News Channel, they were talking about Jesus. After I came home from the discussion time, I turned on the History Channel. Guess what they were talking about? Jesus! In my lifetime such a thing has never happened in America.

A CULTURAL BENCHMARK

It occurred to me that this movie was a kind of cultural benchmark. Most movies come and go without much notice. A movie appears at the local cinema, you read a review, you see an ad, and you decide to go see it. You either like the movie or you don't. Most movies don't change us or get us to think deeply about anything. But now and then a film comes along that forces us to deal with ultimate issues. *The Passion of the Christ* is such a film.

Some Jewish leaders suggested the movie was anti-Semitic. I don't think any of us should dismiss that judgment out of hand. Anti-Semitism is on the rise in many places. I have a book in my library called *Christ-Killers Past and Present*. The author, Jacob Gartenhaus, a Jewish believer in Jesus, recounts the sordid history of Christians who shouted, "Christ-killer" at every Jew they met. He shows persuasively that the Jews as a people were not guilty of crucifying Jesus. So who did? The Apostles' Creed answers this question clearly:

I believe in . . . Jesus Christ, [God's] only Son, our Lord,
who was conceived of the Holy Spirit,
born of the Virgin Mary, suffered under Pontius Pilate.

In light of the questions raised by *The Passion of the Christ*, I'd like to look at this issue from three angles.

HISTORICALLY

It is noteworthy that the Creed passes immediately from the Virgin Birth to the death of Jesus with no mention of anything in between.

There is nothing about his sermons or his miracles. Not a word about Jesus walking on water or confronting the Pharisees or healing the sick. In so doing, the Creed teaches us that Jesus was born to die. The word "suffered" sums up everything that happened between his birth and his death. The Bible never tells us that Jesus smiled or laughed. I'm sure he did, but the Gospels never mention it. Isaiah 53:3 calls him "a man of sorrows, and acquainted with grief." When he was born, Herod tried to kill him (Matthew 2:16-18). When he began his ministry, the people in his hometown took offense at him (Mark 6:3). In the closing hours of his life, he was betrayed by Judas and denied by Peter. His sufferings did not begin on the cross, but it was his suffering that led him to the cross.

His sufferings did not begin on the cross, but it was his suffering that led him to the cross.

Why single out Pontius Pilate? Why not Caiaphas or Herod or Judas or the Roman soldiers or the howling mob? The answer comes from a scene Mel Gibson captured with great power. Jesus has just been scourged. He stands before Pilate, covered with blood, his flesh in tatters, his eyes nearly swollen shut, his face so marred that he barely looks human. Pilate looks at him in shock and pity and in a near-whisper says, "Don't you know I have the power to put to you to death or to free you?" That wasn't a boast—it was a fact. As the Roman governor of Judea, he alone could condemn a man to death. If it is true that many of the Jewish leaders wanted Jesus dead, it's also true that they could do nothing without Pilate's permission. In the end, he must be held accountable for the death of Jesus. If the Jewish leaders loaded the gun, it was Pilate who pulled the trigger.

In the film, and in the Gospels, Pilate comes across as a man who knows that Jesus is innocent, yet lacked the courage to set him free. Twice he said, "I find no guilt in him" (John 19:4, 6). Pilate knew Jesus had committed no crime worthy of death. But like many a politician, he caved in to pressure from his bosses in Rome and from the Jews who wanted Jesus dead. The Truth stood in front of him, but he condemned him to death.

HIS GUILT IS GREATER

Pilate's guilt is greater because he condemned Jesus even though he knew he was innocent.

Both the Bible and the movie make it clear that only some of the Jewish leaders hated the Lord. The Jews as a whole were divided over Jesus—some hated him, some followed him, many were undecided.

From a political point of view, Pontius Pilate was a minor figure in the Roman Empire. Being governor of Judea wasn't like being governor of Texas—it was more like being governor of North Dakota. A Roman governor had two major jobs: collect taxes and keep the peace. Pilate had considerable trouble in that second category. But to the Emperor in Rome, neither Pilate nor the province of Judea mattered very much. It was one tiny spot in a vast empire that stretched across the Mediterranean world. Why mention him at all then? First, because he is the person who condemned Jesus to die. Second, to establish a point in space-time history for the death of Christ. "The reference to Pilate anchors the Creed in history."[14] This means it really happened.

SPIRITUALLY

The fact that Pilate is the person most responsible for the death of Jesus does not end the discussion. As both the movie and the Gospels make clear, there is plenty of guilt to go around. Here's a fact many people don't know. Although Mel Gibson financed, produced, and directed the movie, he appears in only one scene. As Jesus is being nailed to the cross, a man's hand appears, making a fist, holding the nail above Jesus' outstretched palm, showing the soldiers how to do their grisly work. The hand holding the nail belongs to Mel Gibson. It's the only place he appears, and his fist is all you see. He wanted it that way so the world would know that it was his sin that nailed Jesus to the cross. As he said when asked by Diane Sawyer who killed Jesus, "We all did."

By him whose eyes are like a flame of fire, and yet were wet with tears, by him on whose head are many crowns, and who yet wore the crown of thorns, by him who is King of kings and Lord of lords, and yet bowed his head to death for you, resolve that to life's latest breath you will spend and be spent for his praise. (Charles Haddon Spurgeon, THE METROPOLITAN PULPIT TABERNACLE, Sermon #938, "A Good Soldier of Jesus Christ")

Ponder these ancient words from Isaiah 53:4-5: "Surely he has borne our griefs and carried our sorrows; yet we esteemed him stricken, smitten by God, and afflicted. But he was wounded for our transgressions; he was crushed for our iniquities; upon him was the chastisement that brought us peace, and with his stripes we are healed." Four times in these two verses the prophet uses the word "our." "*Our* griefs." "*Our* sorrows." "*Our* transgressions." "*Our iniquities*." It was our sins that nailed Christ to the cross. "And the LORD has laid on him the iniquity of us all" (Isaiah 53:6).

It is said that Bernard of Clairvaux in the twelfth century first penned the words to one of our favorite hymns, "O Sacred Head, Now Wounded." The second verse speaks to our sin and the death of Christ:

> *What thou, my Lord, hast suffered was all for sinners' gain:*
> *Mine, mine was the transgression, but thine the deadly pain.*
> *Lo, here I fall, my Savior! 'Tis I deserve thy place;*
> *Look on me with thy favor, and vouchsafe to me thy grace.*

Our sins have cut us off from God; so we are left to our own feeble devices. Most of us think of ourselves as pretty good people, or at least not as bad as the fellow next door. And it's true that we haven't done every terrible thing that others have done. But our hands are not clean. We have cheated. We have lied. We have gossiped. We have falsely accused. We have made excuses. We have mistreated others.

When we finally get a glimpse of the cross of Christ, we see clearly how great our sin really is.

In the light of Calvary, all our supposed goodness is nothing but filthy rags. The closer you come to Jesus, the more clearly you see your own sin. Isaiah 53 contains the good news we all need. He was bruised for us. He was wounded for us. He was beaten, betrayed, mocked, scourged, crowned with thorns, crucified—all for us. Our sins drove Jesus to the cross, but it was his love for us that kept him there.

In the King James Version, Isaiah 53:6 says, "All we like sheep have gone astray; we have turned every one to his own way; and the LORD hath laid on him the iniquity of us all." Notice that it begins and ends with the word "all." One man gave his testimony this way: "I stooped down low and went in at the first 'all.' Then I stood up straight and walked out at the last 'all.'" The first "all" tells us that we are sinners; the last "all" tells us that Christ has paid the price for our sins.

ULTIMATELY

Who is ultimately responsible for the death of Jesus Christ? The answer may surprise you.

According to the Bible, God takes responsibility for the death of his Son.

The first part of Isaiah 53:10 in the New International Version says, "Yet it was the LORD's will to crush him and cause him to suffer." The New King James gives that phrase a slightly different feel: "Yet it pleased the LORD to bruise Him; He has put Him to grief." Both versions say the same thing, but the NIV emphasizes that it pleased the Lord to "crush" his only Son. As a father of three sons, I cannot fathom that. I cannot imagine willingly putting one of my sons to death, much less taking pleasure in it. But the truth stands and cannot be denied:

Jesus died because his Father willed that he should die.

The terrible suffering our Lord endured did not happen by chance, nor did it happen solely because the Jewish leaders wanted it and Pilate cravenly caved in. Behind the evil deeds of evil men stands the Lord

God Almighty. He and he alone sent Jesus to the cross. Until you understand that fact, the true meaning of the death of Christ will be lost to you. The death of Jesus was God's idea.

"IT ISN'T RIGHT"

Just before the discussion time at our church, after we had seen the film, I asked a young man what he thought about *The Passion of the Christ*. He gripped my hand, his eyes filled with tears, and his lips began to quiver. For a long time he couldn't say anything. Finally, with great emotion, he spoke three words: "It isn't right." The way the soldiers treated Jesus wasn't right. How could such brutality ever be justified? Listen to the answer provided by John Piper in his wonderful book, *The Passion of Jesus Christ*:

> The most important question of the twenty-first century is: Why did Jesus Christ suffer so much? But we will never see the importance if we fail to go beyond human cause. The ultimate answer to the question, Who crucified Jesus? is: God did. It is a staggering thought. Jesus was his Son. And the suffering was unsurpassed. But the whole message of the Bible leads to this conclusion.[15]

No one would have expected God to put his only Son on the cross. But that's exactly what happened. The events of Good Friday will make no sense until you grasp that great truth. But what about Herod and Judas and Caiaphas and Pontius Pilate? What about those who cheered and jeered? What about the incredibly brutal Roman soldiers who beat Christ so savagely that they nearly killed him? Does God's involvement somehow get them off the hook?

The answer comes to us in a prayer from the book of Acts. During a wave of persecution shortly after the church was born, the believers gathered to ask God for his help. Their prayer included this remarkable sentence: "For truly Your holy Servant Jesus, whom You anointed, both Herod and Pontius Pilate, with the Gentiles and the people of Israel, were gathered together to do whatever Your hand and Your

Credo

purpose determined before to be done" (4:27-28, NKJV). Note two facts:
1) *They name names*—Herod and Pilate. The believers didn't forget who
crucified their Lord—and God doesn't forget either. 2) *Those leaders'
evil serves God's greater purposes.* That's why the church affirms that
what those evil men did—and did freely and with no sense of divine
coercion—was what God "determined" (a very strong word) before-
hand should be done. Herod and Pilate are truly guilty, but they did
what God determined should be done. Is there a mystery here? Yes, but
the mystery does not lessen the truth that Pilate and Herod and all the
rest were truly guilty and through their sin God's will regarding Jesus
was accomplished.

THE GREATEST SIN

That's why Jesus could truthfully take responsibility for his own death:
"For this reason my Father loves me, because I lay down my life that I
may take it up again. No one takes it from me, but I lay it down of my
own accord. I have authority to lay it down, and I have authority to
take it up again. This charge I have received from my Father" (John
10:17-18). This serves as one of the main answers to the charge of anti-
Semitism against *The Passion of the Christ*. Mel Gibson has Jesus utter
these words on his way to the cross. No one killed Jesus against his will.
If God had not willed for his Son to die, and if Jesus had not willingly
laid down his life, all the armies of Rome could not have taken his life.

Herod and Pilate (and everyone else involved) were unwitting actors
in the great drama of redemption. They were truly guilty for their sins,
but through their evil, salvation has come to the world. What is the greatest sin in the world? Surely the answer must be, crucifying the Son of
God. Yet here is a mystery and a paradox that becomes a miracle:

*From the great sin has come the greatest blessing for the whole
human race. The bloody death of Jesus opened the door of heaven for
anyone who wishes to enter.*

Let me ask a more personal question: What is the greatest sin any
of us can commit? We cannot literally repeat the sins of those who put

him to death. For us the greatest sin must be ignoring the Son of God. We do this when we say (by our life or by our lips), "Lord Jesus Christ, I know all that you did for me, and it doesn't matter to me at all." But to ignore what Jesus has purchased at so great a cost is to place ourselves in grave spiritual peril. The poet W. H. Auden once imagined what he would have done if he had been present on that first Good Friday. He says most of us wouldn't see ourselves as disciples cowering in fear or feel that we were important enough to play the role of Pontius Pilate or to be part of the Jewish Sanhedrin.

> In my most optimistic mood I see myself as a Hellenized Jew from Alexandria visiting an intellectual friend. We are walking along, engaged in philosophical argument. Our path takes us past the base of Golgotha. Looking up, we see an all too familiar sight—three crosses surrounded by a jeering crowd. Frowning with prim distaste, I say, "It's disgusting the way the mob enjoy such things. Why can't the authorities execute criminals humanely and in private by giving them hemlock to drink, as they did with Socrates?" Then, averting my eyes from the disagreeable spectacle, I resume our fascinating discussion about the nature of the True, the Good, and the Beautiful.[16]

To ignore what Jesus has purchased at so great a cost is to place ourselves in grave spiritual peril.

No, we're not the sadistic Roman guards, and we're not the frenzied mob. We're not even party-boy Herod or pensive Pilate. Auden has us dead to rights. We're like the educated elite who find the whole spectacle distasteful and unfit for public consumption. In a way we're worse than Pilate or Herod or Caiaphas. At least they cared enough to take a side. We don't want to be involved at all.

I CRUCIFIED MY LORD

I return again to the movie, thinking about what it has meant to me. At the end of my ruminations three things remain: First, *there are scenes of unspeakable horror.* Perhaps this is too much for some people, as it was for many of the critics. Second, *it had to happen the way the Bible describes it.* Jesus prays to his Father because he knows that these things have been appointed for him from the foundation of the universe. As a man, he struggles. As the Son of God, he accepts the Father's will. Third, *I see (perhaps for the first time in a long time) that I am guilty of crucifying my Lord.* My sins nailed him to the cross. My hands are not free of innocent blood. Like Pilate, I wash them but to no avail. The stain remains forever.

A man who saw the scourging scene said he could barely watch it. The torture seemed to go on forever. He found that he could only endure it by saying to himself after each blow hit Jesus, "That one was for me." What they did to Jesus was a monstrous injustice. But before we condemn others, let's ask one question: Who did this? Don't blame the Jews. Don't blame the Romans. If you want to blame anyone, look in the mirror. *You* did it. *I* did it. *We* did it. And Jesus endured it all for us. The lash, the beatings, the crown of thorns, the bruises, the ridicule, the nails, the spear, the desertion, the betrayal—God planned the whole thing. Jesus did it all for you and for me.

At the beginning of the film words from Isaiah 53:5 fill the screen: "He was wounded for our transgressions." The end of that verse adds a wonderful truth, "With his stripes we are healed." There is no sin too great for God. Jesus' blood is more powerful than any evil.

I return to the discussion session at my church one final time. Before we started, a woman tugged at my sleeve and said she wanted to tell me how the film made her feel. She summed it up in one word: "unworthy." That's a good place for all of us to start our spiritual journey.

To return to the hymn "O Sacred Head, Now Wounded":

> *What language shall I borrow*
> *To thank thee, dearest Friend,*
> *For this, thy dying sorrow,*
> *Thy pity without end?*

O make me thine forever;
And should I fainting be,
Lord, let me never, never
Outlive my love to thee.

We do live in amazing times when the world wants to know why Jesus died. The Creed tells us that he "suffered under Pontius Pilate." It will be good if millions of people ponder the meaning of his suffering on the cross.

THINK ABOUT IT!

1. Who killed Jesus? How would you personally answer that question? Be honest. Explain your answer.

2. Do you find it easy or difficult to believe that Jesus was wounded for your transgressions, that he took your place and received the punishment for your sins? Why?

3. What does the statement that "it was the will of the LORD to crush [Jesus]" mean to you? How could the Heavenly Father possibly derive pleasure from his Son's being killed? What does this mean to you personally?

8

The Day God Died:
"Crucified, Died"

When Christ had offered for all time a single sacrifice for sins, he sat down at the right hand of God.

HEBREWS 10:12

The Apostles' Creed contains four phrases that refer to the death of Jesus Christ:

- crucified
- died
- buried
- descended into hell

This may seem redundant, especially in a Creed that presents the entire Christian faith in approximately 110 words. Why are six words used to describe the death of Christ when one would have told the story—"died." What additional truth is added by the piling up of phrases relating to his death?

Why does the Creed describes the death of Christ in four different ways? Throughout the history of the Christian church critics and skeptics have attacked Christianity by claiming that Jesus never rose from the dead. For example, in the early church the Gnostics claimed that Jesus did not literally die. They said the Spirit of God entered Jesus at his baptism and left before his crucifixion.

Hundreds of years later the prophet Mohammed founded the

religion of Islam, which teaches that Jesus only *appeared* to die. Muslim scholars differ over what exactly happened to Jesus. Some say that at the last second another person took his place on the cross—perhaps Judas, perhaps Simon of Cyrene. They suggest that God cast a spell over the enemies of Jesus so the switch could take place without them knowing it. That's a clever idea with absolutely no basis in historical fact.

Some writers speculate that Jesus fainted or swooned or passed out from the beatings and the crucifixion, and the disciples, the Jews, and the Romans just thought he was dead when they took his body down from the cross. Later when his body was placed in the cool tomb, he revived, regained his strength, somehow rolled the massive stone away, and walked out on Sunday morning looking fresh, healthy, strong, and totally recovered—so much so that his disciples mistakenly thought he had risen from the dead. That theory is both ingenious and preposterous. If you understand the brutal nature of crucifixion, you must conclude that it takes more faith to believe that than to believe that Jesus actually died and rose from the dead.

THE CERTAINTY OF HIS DEATH

I often find myself drawn to Isaiah 53—the greatest Old Testament description of our Lord's death. That chapter emphasizes God's activity in the events surrounding the crucifixion. It was the Lord who laid on Jesus the sins of us all. Isaiah 53:10 says that the Lord was pleased to crush his own Son. What sort of father would be pleased to crush his son? (We talked about this earlier but need to touch on it briefly again here.) Either the father hates his own son and wishes to see him suffer, or the father understands that the suffering is necessary to gain some greater good that cannot come any other way.

The Father ordains the death of his Son so that salvation might come to the world. And the Son willingly goes as a lamb to the slaughter.

In the case of Christ, the Father ordains the death of his Son so that salvation might come to the world. And the Son willingly goes as a lamb to the slaughter. He endures the cross and despises the shame, looking to the joy that will come later through the redemption of the world (Hebrews 12:2). He enters the crucible of eternal pain because in the end, "when he sees all that is accomplished by his anguish, he will be satisfied" (Isaiah 53:11, NLT).

What happened to Jesus did not happen by accident or even by a random combination of circumstances. All of it came to pass by God's predetermined plan.

Jesus Christ was crucified because God willed that his Son be crucified. He died because God willed it to be so. He was buried because God ordained that his Son be buried. He fully entered into the realm of death not by accident, but by divine design. The writers of the Apostles' Creed understood this, and that's why they used four phrases to describe his death.

Did Jesus Really Die?

The New Testament offers a clear, unambiguous answer. First, *Jesus repeatedly predicted his own death.* In Matthew 20:18-19 he told his disciples, "See, we are going up to Jerusalem. And the Son of Man will be delivered over to the chief priests and scribes, and they will condemn him to death and deliver him over to the Gentiles to be mocked and flogged and crucified, and he will be raised on the third day." Nothing that happened to Jesus was a surprise to him. He knew it was part of the Father's plan for him and warned his disciples about what would happen to him in Jerusalem.

Second, *Pilate delivered Jesus over to be crucified.* Although he tried to wash his hands of any guilt, he could not wash the blood of Jesus away. The crowd wanted Jesus dead, and he gave in to their hatred and bloodlust.

Third, *the Romans designed crucifixion as a particularly terrible way to die.* Over the centuries the Romans developed a number of ways to kill people. Of the various options, crucifixion was the worst, reserved for the most heinous criminals and for traitors against the state. It is said that the Romans crucified 250,000 Jews. On some occasions the Romans crucified hundreds of people at a time. Some men would hang on the cross in agony for twenty-four, forty-eight, or even seventy-two hours—exposed to the elements, to wild animals, to birds that might peck their eyes out and exposed to passers-by who would taunt them as their loved ones watched in horror.

Fourth, *the Romans scourged Jesus as part of the preparation for crucifixion.* This involved beating him with wooden rods and with leather belts embedded with pieces of stone, metal, and glass. The beating not only weakened the victim, it lacerated him until his flesh hung in tatters.

Fifth, *the centurions declared that Jesus was already dead, which is why they didn't break his bones.* The centurions were professional soldiers who didn't care about Jesus one way or the other. They were just doing their job, and they did it well. They knew the difference between a coma and death. After all Jesus had been through, they knew he could not possibly be alive. They knew without a doubt that he was dead.

Sixth, *the soldiers pierced his side with a spear to be absolutely certain he was dead.* Most authorities believe the water and blood that gushed forth came from the sac around Jesus' heart, another proof he had truly died.

Seventh, *the women prepared his body for burial following accepted Jewish practices.* This involved cleaning the body (a difficult job because of Jesus' many wounds), wrapping it tightly with a linen cloth, and sprinkling spices and aromatic resins between the linen wrappings. The spices and resins hardened to form a kind of cocoon around the dead body both to preserve it and to deter grave robbers.

Eighth, *the tomb was sealed with an enormous boulder weighing three to five tons.*

Ninth, *the Roman guards at the tomb ensured that no one could steal the body.* Think about it—these men weren't pushovers but professional soldiers.

Tenth, *on Saturday night the Romans, the Jewish leaders, and the disciples agreed on only one point—Jesus was dead.* No one believed for a moment that he had somehow survived the beating, the scourging, the crown of thorns, the severe blood loss, the exhaustion, the crucifixion, the exposure, the incredible physical suffering, and the gradual collapse of all his bodily systems. Jesus died in public, outside the walls of Jerusalem, surrounded by soldiers who had seen many men die, with his mother nearby, the Jewish leaders watching, and a large crowd of onlookers. No one could have faked his own death in that situation. Jesus was truly dead. The evidence is overwhelming.

THE SIGNIFICANCE OF HIS DEATH

Six verses from Hebrews 9—10 reveal the true significance of Jesus' death.

No blood, no forgiveness. "Without the shedding of blood there is no forgiveness of sins" (Hebrews 9:22).

Animal blood won't do. "It is impossible for the blood of bulls and goats to take away sins" (Hebrews 10:4).

Jesus sacrificed himself for us. "He has appeared once for all at the end of the ages to put away sin by the sacrifice of himself" (Hebrews 9:26).

His sacrifice takes away our sin. "Christ, having been offered once to bear the sins of many . . ." (Hebrews 9:28).

There is only one sacrifice for sin. "Christ had offered for all time a single sacrifice for sins" (Hebrews 10:12).

His sacrifice makes us holy. "For by a single offering he has perfected for all time those who are being sanctified" (Hebrews 10:14).

Thus we see the centrality of the cross.

Start anywhere in the Bible, and the result is the same—all roads lead inexorably to the cross. Since sin is the ultimate problem of the human race, the cross is God's ultimate answer.

Start anywhere in the Bible, and the result is the same—all roads lead inexorably to the cross.

- There is one sacrifice for sin—and only one.
- That sacrifice was offered once for all time—never to be repeated.
- Jesus offered himself to take away sin—no one else could do what he did.
- His sacrifice solves the sin problem—there is no other solution.
- His sacrifice makes us holy—there is no other way to be holy.

The death of Jesus Christ is therefore the most important event in world history.

Nothing else that has ever happened has had the impact of the cross of Jesus Christ. We see this in our own day. Mel Gibson made a movie about the death of Jesus, and people couldn't stop talking about it!

To evangelize is to spread the good news that Jesus Christ died for our sins and was raised from the dead according to the Scriptures, and that as the reigning Lord he now offers the forgiveness of sins and the liberating gift of the Spirit to all who repent and believe. (Lausanne Covenant, International Congress on World Evangelization, 1974)

Nothing But the Blood of Jesus

Let's wrap things up with three statements of application:

- *God only has one plan of salvation for the whole human race.*
- *There is only one way to heaven—Jesus Christ our Lord.*
- *There is only one sacrifice that can take away our sin and make us holy.*

One plan, one way, one man, one sacrifice. The writer of Hebrews repeats these themes over and over. Jesus was offered once for all as God's perfect sacrifice that takes away our sin. He alone can make us holy. In case we miss the point, Hebrews 10 even quotes a famous passage (famous to first-century Jews at least) from Jeremiah 31, where God promises two wonderful gifts to his people: "This is the covenant that I will make with them after those days, declares the Lord: I will put my laws on their hearts, and write them on their minds. . . . I will remember their sins and their lawless deeds no more" (Hebrews

10:16-17). Since this may not be as clear to us as it was to the original readers, let me lay it out this way:

Jeremiah 31 (written five hundred years before the birth of Christ) is quoted in Hebrews 10 (written around A.D. 65) to help us understand what the cross of Christ (A.D. 33) means in the twenty-first century.

The whole point is that the death of Christ procures two things for us we could not get any other way:

• A brand-new heart (the law written in our hearts).

• Total forgiveness (God remembers our sins no more).

And that's why Hebrews 10:18 tells us that where sin is forgiven (through the death of Christ), "there is no longer any offering for sin." Jesus has done everything necessary for your sins to be forgiven. If his death is not enough for you, there isn't a Plan B. God doesn't say, "If you don't like what my Son did for you, how about some animal sacrifices? Maybe you'd like to be a Hindu or a Buddhist and see if that works out." If you refuse to come to Christ as Lord and Savior, then the door of heaven will remain shut to you.

If Jesus' death is not enough for you, there isn't a Plan B. If you refuse to come to Christ as Lord and Savior, then the door of heaven will remain shut to you.

Now that Jesus has died, no other sacrifice is necessary. No other will be accepted. Without his death, there is no forgiveness, no salvation, and no hope of heaven.

Do you want to go to heaven? If the answer is yes, here are three things you need to know. First, *you can't do it on your own.* You can try, but you will die trying. You cannot make your own way to heaven. Second, *God has done it for you.* This is the wonderful, life-saving good news of the gospel. What you could not do for yourself, God has done for you through Jesus Christ, his only Son. In his bloody death on the cross, Jesus paid the full price for your sins. That's what he meant when he cried out, "It is finished" (John 19:30). The work of salvation has been completed. The price has been paid. The heavy blows of judgment fell on the Lamb of God.

Third, *when you come to Jesus by faith, your sins are forgiven forever.* A few years ago a Nigerian pastor gave me a hymnbook entitled *Sacred Songs and Solos.* When you open to the title page, you find that it was compiled by Ira Sankey (D. L. Moody's songleader) in the late 1800s. This hymnbook—though very old—is still used by the churches of Nigeria and contains many unfamiliar hymns. But some of them are gems. These are the words to number 142:

> *Nothing either great or small—*
> *Nothing, sinner, no.*
> *Jesus did it, did it all,*
> *Long, long ago.*

> *"It is finished!" yes, indeed.*
> *Finished every jot:*
> *Sinner, this is all you need—*
> *Tell me, is it not?*

> *When He, from His lofty throne,*
> *Stooped to do and die,*
> *Everything was fully done:*
> *Hearken to His cry.*

> *Weary, working, burdened one,*
> *Wherefore toil you so?*
> *Cease your doing; all was done*
> *Long, long ago.*

> *Till to Jesus' work you cling*
> *By a simple faith,*
> *"Doing" is a deadly thing—*
> *"Doing" leads to death.*

Cast your deadly "doing" down—
Down at Jesus' feet;
Stand in Him, in Him alone,
Gloriously complete.

They don't write many hymns like that nowadays. Consider these two lines: "Cease your doing; all was done / Long, long ago." It's true. "All was done" when Jesus cried, "It is finished." It was finished then, it is finished now, and to the glory of God, after a million times a million years have passed, it will still be finished.

As the hymn says, "Sinner, this is all you need— / Tell me, is it not?"

THINK ABOUT IT!

1. Why is it important to recognize that Jesus really did die, that he didn't just pass out or allow someone else to take his place but actually experienced death? Why does this matter?

2. Why was Jesus able to be our substitute and a sacrifice for our sins? Why was it necessary for him to die?

3. Are you convinced that Jesus was the only one who could bring us forgiveness, that only his sacrifice could atone for our sins? Why or why not? Have you personally received him as your own Savior from sin? If not, will you do so today?

9

God's Scapegoat:
"Buried"

*We were buried therefore with him . . . in order that, just as
Christ was raised from the dead by the glory of the Father,
we too might walk in newness of life.*

R O M A N S   6 : 4

As we have seen, the Apostles' Creed confesses, "I believe
in . . . Jesus Christus . . . who . . . suffered under Pontius Pilate, was crucified, died, and was buried."

The word *buried* doesn't seem necessary. We know Jesus died.
We know he rose from the dead. If we know Jesus died for our sins
and rose on the third day, of course he was buried in between. In a
Creed in which words are used sparingly, in which whole areas of
doctrine are either assumed or passed over in silence, in which the
whole of Christ's teaching ministry and all of his miracles are not
even mentioned, why does the Creed say he was "buried"? Why
state the obvious?

When we read the story of Jesus' life, we tend to go straight from
his death to his resurrection, as if nothing important happened in
between. But the Creed forces us to stop and take another look at the
biblical text. The simple word "buried" tells us more than what happened to the body of Jesus. It alerts us to an area of biblical truth that
we might otherwise overlook.

Credo

THREE KEY PASSAGES

Isaiah 53 contains the most extensive Old Testament prophecy concerning the death of our Lord, and verse 9 contains an explicit reference to his burial, seven hundred years before Christ was born. "And they made his grave with the wicked and with a rich man in his death, although he had done no violence, and there was no deceit in his mouth." Since the Romans reserved crucifixion for the worst criminals and for enemies of the state, they would throw dead bodies taken down from the cross into a ditch or onto a pile of burning garbage. No doubt the Jewish leaders who hated Jesus had "assigned" (NIV) this fate to him in their minds. But he ended up being buried in a rich man's tomb.

First Corinthians 15:1-6 contains a concise summary of the gospel: "Now I would remind you, brothers, of the gospel I preached to you" (v. 1). Then he goes on to spell out the gospel in verses 3-5: "For I delivered to you as of first importance what I also received: that Christ died for our sins in accordance with the Scriptures, that he was buried, that he was raised on the third day in accordance with the Scriptures, and that he appeared to Cephas, then to the twelve." Notice how clearly he lays out the gospel message:

- He was crucified.
- *He was buried.*
- He was raised on the third day.
- He appeared.

Paul regarded the burial of Jesus as an essential part of the gospel message.

Matthew 26:6-13 records the story of Mary's anointing Jesus' head with a jar of very expensive perfume. When John (chapter 12) told the same story, he added the fact that Mary also anointed Jesus' feet with a pint of "pure nard" (v. 3), an extremely costly perfume imported from India. It would have cost a year's wages to buy a pint of that perfume, and Mary poured it all on Jesus' head and feet. When the disciples (led by Judas) protested her wasteful actions, Jesus defended Mary: "In pouring this ointment on my body, she has done it to prepare me for burial. Truly, I say to you, wherever this gospel is proclaimed in the whole world, what she has done will also be told in memory of her" (vv. 12-13). In her extravagant expression of love, Mary was doing more than she knew: What she was doing on that Saturday in Bethany would be done to the dead body of Jesus the following Friday when he was taken down from the cross. The phrase "this gospel" tells us again that the burial of Jesus is part of the gospel message. And that's why it appears in the Apostles' Creed.

The burial of Jesus is part of the gospel message.

HIS BURIAL EXPLAINED

The details of Jesus' burial appear in all four Gospels: Matthew 27:57-61; Mark 15:42-47; Luke 23:50-56; John 19:38-42. Rather than look at each passage individually, I'd like to combine them into one seamless account.

The story begins late on Friday afternoon outside the city walls of Jerusalem. Jesus was dead by 3:00 P.M. Sundown (marking the beginning of the Jewish Sabbath) began at 6:00 P.M. For some period of time after his death, his corpse hung on the cross, suspended by ropes and the spikes in his hands and feet. Eventually a man named Joseph of Arimathea stepped forward. All that we know about him comes from the four Gospels. He was rich, righteous, and a member of the Jewish ruling council, the Sanhedrin. That meant he would have been highly respected and well-known to many people. The Gospels tell us he was a wise man and a counselor who was looking for the Kingdom of God. They also tell us that he had cast his vote against the death of Jesus. But the most important fact was not known to others on the ruling council: Joseph was a secret believer in Jesus. Although we don't know how it happened, he had become convinced that Jesus was the Messiah of Israel, the Son of God and the Son of Man, the fulfillment of the prophecies of the Old Testament. If others had known, he would have faced harassment and ridicule.

Mark tells us that Joseph "took courage and went to Pilate" to ask for Jesus' body (15:43). Pilate had no use for the Jewish leaders, and they had no use for him. Joseph could not have known how Pilate would respond at that crucial moment, but he went to him anyway. Pilate's first response was surprise that Jesus was dead. Normally men lasted longer than six hours on the cross. Certainly this was partly due to the savage treatment Jesus had received. But the greater explanation is this:

He was not killed. He laid down his life voluntarily.

Pilate summoned the centurion on duty at the cross and asked if Jesus had already died. Then he gave Joseph permission to take the body of Jesus down from the cross. At this point John adds a fact that the other Gospel writers don't mention. Joseph was joined in his task by another secret disciple, Nicodemus. John 3 tells how Nicodemus (who was also a member of the ruling council) came to Jesus at night, for fear that others would know of his visit. Jesus told him he needed to be "born again" or "born from above." Sometime between that night and Good Friday, Nicodemus had become a secret follower of our Lord. The two men who took care of Jesus' body were Jewish leaders who were also secret believers.

Messy Business

Taking the body down was a difficult, messy business. Blood oozed from cuts and lacerations, there was an open wound in his side from the spear, and there were holes in his hands and his feet. His face had been beaten almost beyond recognition. After cleaning the body, Joseph and Nicodemus began to wrap it tightly with a linen cloth. John tells us that they interspersed seventy-five pounds of aloes and myrrh with the linen as it wrapped around his body (19:39). This aromatic ointment would eventually harden into a nearly impenetrable shell.

The two men had to hurry because according to Jewish law, they could not handle a dead body on the Sabbath. Their work would have taken the better part of two hours. So now it is past 5:00 P.M. They have less than sixty minutes to finish burying Jesus, when the Sabbath would begin. In one of the God-ordained serendipities of this story, Joseph had purchased a tomb that had recently been hewn from the rock. No doubt he had intended to use it as the burial place for himself and his wife and possibly other members of his family.

If you ever go to the Holy Land, your tour guide will take you to a place called Gordon's Calvary outside the Damascus Gate. It's a limestone outcropping that the weather has carved into what might be the shape of a skull. Many people think this is where Jesus was crucified. Next to it—literally only a few yards away—is the Garden Tomb, a peaceful, restful location with a first-century tomb cut into a hillside. There is even a trough in front of the tomb where the stone would have been rolled in front of the entrance. I've been inside that tomb three times. There is a chamber for visitors and a chamber where the body would be placed. Many people think this is where our Lord's body was buried on Good Friday. If not, he was buried someplace very similar. I should add that having visited the Garden Tomb three times, I can testify that the tomb is empty. Whoever was buried there left a long time ago.

There was no limit to Christ's self-giving for us. His death marks His total self-giving in that act of love that redeems us. That is how much He values us. He gives everything He has and everything He is for us. That thought must allow us to walk tall, secure in the fatherly love of God. (Joanna and Alister McGrath, SELF-ESTEEM: THE CROSS AND CHRISTIAN CONFIDENCE)

It was now only a few minutes before 6:00 P.M. Joseph and Nicodemus picked up the lifeless corpse of Jesus and half-carried, half-dragged it to the garden tomb. Thank goodness it wasn't far away. Between the weight of the body and the linen and spices it must have weighed almost 250 pounds. Meanwhile, the sun slowly sank into the western horizon. The two secret disciples carried Jesus' body to the tomb. Close behind were Mary Magdalene and the other Mary, weep-ing. The entrance to the tomb was very small. Nicodemus and Joseph had to bend over to get inside. Inside, the tomb was almost pitch-black, musty, and damp. They laid the body of Jesus on a ledge. When they got outside, Joseph and Nicodemus rolled a great stone over the entrance. The women sat by the side watching.

Then Joseph and Nicodemus left. Later the two Marys left. Darkness fell on the garden cemetery. Inside the tomb there was silence. The smell of death was everywhere.

Why So Much Detail?

To prove that he really died. This was a huge issue in the early church—and remains so to this very day. The details of his burial reinforce the central truth that Jesus truly died on the cross.

To show the true cost of our salvation. Jesus was buried because he died carrying the heavy burden of our guilt and shame. His burial shows us the true end of our rebellion and lawlessness. Left to ourselves, we end up in the grave—which is where our Lord ended up after he had suffered for our sins.

To teach us that God does not forsake us when we die. We know that "precious in the sight of the LORD is the death of his saints" (Psalm 116:15). Yet death seems anything but precious to us. It is dark, cold, frightening. We fear death because it cuts us off from the land of the living. It pleased the Father to crush his only Son (Isaiah 53:10). Yet in that crushing, God did not abandon him forever. The ministrations of Joseph and Nicodemus and the kind care of the sorrowing women were God's way of saying, "I have not forsaken my Son in his death."

We learn from this that burying the dead is a Christian duty and a Christian service to our loved ones. If God cared enough for his Son to see that he was properly buried, we should do the same for those we love.

To sanctify death so that we will not be afraid to die. Here we come even closer to the heart of the gospel. Is there any fear more fundamental than the fear of death? But Jesus has transformed death for those who follow him. What happens to us, happened first to him. And what happened to him will one day happen to us. He entered death's dark realm and conquered it once and for all. By his victory over death he has sanctified it so that we no longer need to fear it. Thus we will not fear the tomb, knowing that one day by God's grace, like Jesus, we too will come out.

> **Is there any fear more fundamental than the fear of death? But Jesus has transformed death for those who follow him.**

To picture the complete removal of our sins. We know that Jesus died so that our sins might be forgiven. But we often overlook an aspect of this truth. John the Baptist said of Jesus, "Behold, the Lamb of God, who takes away the sins of the world!" (John 1:29). One of the primary Hebrew words for forgiveness means "to lift and take away." God removes the burden of our sin, and then he takes it far, far away.

HIS BURIAL ILLUSTRATED

We see an illustration of this in the story of the Day of Atonement in Leviticus 16. On one day each year—Yom Kippur, the Day of Atonement—the high priest (and only the high priest) would go behind the thick veil to enter the Most Holy Place. That most sacred spot in ancient Judaism contained the Ark of the Covenant, which was a small, ornate chest with a golden lid called the mercy seat.

On that one day of the year, two goats were brought before the high priest. One was chosen by lot for sacrifice. After that goat was killed, the high priest carried its blood into the Most Holy Place and sprinkled it on the mercy seat, signifying that blood had been shed for the sins of the people. Then when the high priest came out of the tabernacle to stand before the people, the second goat was brought to him. Placing his hands on it, he prayed a prayer of confession, naming the sins of the people of Israel. You can imagine the tension as he called out the sins of the people:

- adultery
- fornication
- uncleanness
- immorality
- impurity
- theft
- profanity
- bitterness
- hatred
- malice
- murder
- greed
- lust
- envy
- pride
- jealousy
- oath-breaking

On and on the list would go, until all the hearers were convicted of their own sinfulness. A man then took the goat—called the scapegoat—and led it into the wilderness. He walked until he was far out of sight of the Jews, in a distant, desolate corner of the wilderness. Only then did he release the scapegoat, allowing it to wander off on its own. Thus God demonstrated that he not only forgives sins, he removes them from us so far that they can never come back again.

Not just forgiven. But forgiven and removed forever.

HIS BURIAL APPLIED

- When Christ went into the tomb, he carried our sins with him.
- When he came out of the tomb, our sins were gone forever.

When John Bunyan wrote the classic *Pilgrim's Progress*, he included a section that perfectly describes this truth. The book itself is an allegory of a pilgrim named Christian who makes his journey from earth to heaven. But early in the story he carries the burden of his own sins. This is how he is set free:

He ran thus till he came at a place somewhat ascending; and upon that place stood a cross, and a little below, in the bottom, a sepulcher. So I saw in my dream, that just as Christian came up with the cross, his burden loosed from off his shoulders, and fell from off his back, and began to tumble, and so continued to do till it came to the mouth of the sepulcher, where it fell in, and I saw it no more.

When our sins are forgiven and removed, we see them no more.

The burden is not only "lifted at Calvary," as a gospel song says, but it is rolled away so we will never have to carry it again.

In 1910 an evangelist named J. Wilbur Chapman (he was one of Billy Sunday's mentors) wrote a gospel song that traces the story of Christ's life from his birth through his life, death, resurrection, and second coming. The song is called "One Day," and the chorus goes like this:

> *Living, He loved me; dying, He saved me;*
> *Buried, He carried my sins far away;*
> *Rising, He justified freely, forever;*
> *One day He's coming—O glorious day!*

That second line connects the burial of Jesus with the complete removal of our sins. Jesus is the great Scapegoat who stands in our place, bearing our sins, taking them far away. Have you laid the burden of your sin on Jesus? Rejoice in your deliverance from sin, and adore the Redeemer who paid the price and took the heavy load, who went to the cross and then to the grave so that you might be set free.

THINK ABOUT IT!

1. In your own words, why did the authors of the Apostles' Creed include the word "buried"? Is it unnecessary or redundant? Why or why not?

2. Why do you think Joseph of Arimathea and Nicodemus stepped forward to bury Jesus? What risks were they taking? Would you have done the same? Why or why not?

3. What's the connection between Jesus' burial and the removal of our sins when we believe in him as our personal Savior? What does this mean to you? Share this with one other person today.

10

The Strangest Part of the Creed: "He Descended into Hell"

[God] disarmed the rulers and authorities and put them to open shame, by triumphing over them in [Christ].

COLOSSIANS 2:15

What happened to Jesus between his death and resurrection? We know his body was buried, but what about his spirit? Where was he and what was he doing between his death at 3:00 P.M. on Friday and his resurrection sometime before sunrise on Sunday morning? The short answer is, we don't know for sure. The Bible offers some clues, but it's impossible to be dogmatic.

We begin with the answer offered by the Apostles' Creed: Jesus "descended into hell." The very moment we say those words, a host of questions arise. In what sense did Jesus "descend" into hell? When did this happen? And what "hell" did he descend into? What does the phrase mean? Why is it in the Creed? Is it biblical? Do we believe it? If we don't believe it, why do we say it? On that last point, we can observe that not every version of the Apostles' Creed and not every church that recites it includes this phrase.

So the phrase itself provokes controversy. Here are two other facts to consider. *The Bible nowhere explicitly says that Jesus descended into hell.* That doesn't mean it's not true or that we shouldn't say it, but it does mean we can't find a verse that says, "Jesus descended into hell."

Early versions of the Creed (say around A.D. 150-200) omit this phrase. It didn't appear until approximately two hundred and fifty to three hundred years later. Eventually it became a standard part of the Creed, and it appears in most versions today. But the debate over its meaning and biblical foundation continues. Scholars have argued about this phrase for more than two thousand years, and they continue to argue about it today.

Later in this chapter I will explain why I believe the phrase is both biblical and spiritually helpful. For the moment, let's notice how the Creed uses a certain verb form to describe Jesus Christ. Most of the phrases are in the passive voice: He "was conceived . . . [was] born . . . was crucified . . . was buried." These verbs describe things that happened to Christ or were done to him by others. But when the Creed comes to this phrase, it switches to the active voice: "He descended into hell."

Whatever else it means, this phrase tells us that Jesus did this of his own initiative.

He who was the highest left heaven, came to earth, and in his death and burial descended to the lowest depths of the universe. By using the active voice, the writers of the Creed make a strong statement about what Jesus did. Whatever the phrase "He descended into hell" means, it didn't happen by accident but by our Lord's divine design. Wherever he went and whatever he did there, he went there on purpose.

> He who was the highest left heaven, came to earth, and in his death and burial descended to the lowest depths of the universe.

PSALM 139:7-8

"Where shall I go from your Spirit? Or where shall I flee from your presence? If I ascend to heaven, you are there! If I make my bed in Sheol [NIV, "in the depths"], you are there." The King James Version translates "Sheol" as "hell": "If I make my bed in hell, thou art there." The early verses of Psalm 139 assure us of God's omnipresence—wherever we go, he is already there. There is no part of the universe—no matter how low or how dark or how distant it may be—where he is not now and always present.

COLOSSIANS 2:15

"[God] disarmed the rulers and authorities and put them to open shame, by triumphing over them in [Christ]." The phrase "rulers and authorities" refers to the spiritual forces of wickedness, not to human rulers. By his bloody death on the cross, Christ triumphed over Satan and his demons in all their various ranks and titles. The cross was a decisive victory for the Son of God.

He won the battle so convincingly that the outcome of the war can no longer be in doubt.

To "disarm" someone means to take his weapons away. When Jesus died on the cross, he took spiritual guns and ammo out of the hands of the demons and publicly humiliated them. Picture the Roman legions returning from a successful war. As they enter the city, vast throngs of women and children line the streets. On and on they march, a seemingly endless parade. Then come the victorious generals, each one accompanied by singers, dancers, and musicians. Finally at the end of the procession you spot a long line of weary, dirty, emaciated men, their hands tied—defeated soldiers on display as proof of Rome's invincible power.

When Jesus died, something stupendous happened in the spiritual realm.

Although this was invisible to the naked eye, it was seen by all the angels and the Old Testament saints. They watched as Jesus, like some conquering Old West hero, entered the infernal regions and disarmed the bad guys one by one. Then he marched them in full view of his Heavenly Father so every created being would know that he had won the victory.

Jesus, like some conquering Old West hero, entered the infernal regions and disarmed the bad guys one by one.

1 PETER 3:18-19

"For Christ also suffered once for sins, the righteous for the unrighteous, that he might bring us to God, being put to death in the flesh but made alive in the spirit, in which he went and proclaimed to the spirits in prison." One of my seminary professors called 1 Peter 3:18-22 the most difficult passage in the New Testament. It's not difficult to translate the words per se, but it is extraordinarily difficult to understand what they mean. What exactly was Peter trying to say? One evangelical commentator noted that there are nine Greek words in verse 19—and scholars disagree about the meaning of all of them!

It's fair to say that no one is certain about what Peter means, even though some people *think* they know. Verse 18 is clear as it stands. It's a simple statement of substitutionary atonement: Christ died on our behalf to bring us to God. But he continued in verse 19 by talking about Jesus being dead in the flesh and made alive by the Spirit. The NIV capitalizes the word "Spirit" so we would know that Peter means the Holy Spirit. But many commentators and some translations, including the ESV (I lean in this direction), prefer to use a lower-case s—"spirit"—meaning Christ's human spirit.

Then Peter says Christ went and preached to "the spirits in prison." After canvassing the various options, I personally think he means that Christ preached or proclaimed his victory to the imprisoned spirit beings—demons who rebelled against God. I say *think* because I'm expressing an opinion, not a certainty. And I'm not even going to go into the part about Noah, the ark, and baptism (vv. 20-21). That can wait for another book!

TOTALLY DEAD

Three Bible words will help us think about the phrase "he descended into hell." First, there is the Hebrew word *sheol*. A very common word in the Old Testament, it refers to the shadowy realm of the dead. Sometimes it is translated as "grave." Second, there is the Greek word *hades*, which to us means "hell" but in the New Testament is the equivalent of the Hebrew word *sheol*. Third, there is the Greek word *gehenna*, which always refers to the place we call hell, the place of fire and brimstone, everlasting torment. The word *gehenna* comes from the enormous trash dump in the Hinnom Valley outside Jerusalem. Smoke and fire ascended there day and night. It became a symbol for hell, the place of eternal suffering.

How does this apply to the Apostles' Creed? When we hear that Jesus "descended into hell," we automatically think of the word *gehenna*—the place of fire, smoke, and suffering. But that's almost certainly *not* what the writers of the Creed meant. They were not trying to say that Jesus entered the burning flames of hell. When the Creed uses the word "hell," the real meaning is closer to *sheol* or *hades*. The Creed is telling us that when Jesus died, he fully entered the realm of the dead.

He was truly and utterly and completely dead from a human point of view.

In one person he (Christ) joins God and humankind together; and being united to us who were cursed, he was made a curse for us and hid his blessing in our sin, in our death, and in our curse, which condemned him and put him to death. But because he was the Son of God, he could not be held by the curse and death but overcame them, led them captive, and triumphed over them. (Martin Luther, GALATIANS)

You may recall a scene in the movie *The Princess Bride*. The handsome hero has apparently died, but he is taken to Mad Max, a local magician who assures his friends that the hero is only "mostly dead." That was good news for the hero because there is a huge difference between "mostly dead" and "totally dead." But when Jesus died, he was *totally* dead. He was not spared the pains of death in any way. That's the point the Creed is making.

With all of that as background, let's consider what this strange phrase can't mean, what it might mean, and what it must mean.

WHAT IT CAN'T MEAN

It can't mean that Jesus offered salvation to those who were already dead. Nothing in the Bible supports postmortem salvation. Now is the day of salvation (2 Corinthians 6:1-2). Today is the day when we must trust Christ as Savior. "It is appointed for man to die once, and after that comes judgment" (Hebrews 9:27). The only chance we have to accept Christ is when we are alive. Once we die, we must stand before God for judgment. And once a person goes to hell, he will stay there forever.

Now is the day of salvation (2 Corinthians 6:1-2). Today is the day when we must trust Christ as Savior.

Second, *this phrase cannot mean that Jesus burned in the flames of hell.* The very idea is revolting and without biblical foundation. Jesus suffered the penalty for our sins when he died on the cross, not after his body was buried.

Third, *this phrase can't mean that Jesus did anything between his death and resurrection that added to his work on the cross.* When Jesus said, "It is finished," he meant the work of salvation had been completely accomplished, and the price for sin had been paid in full. Nothing could ever be added to the value of what he did on the cross.

WHAT IT MIGHT MEAN

In the Middle Ages various writers developed an elaborate doctrine called "the harrowing of hell." Many people believed that between his crucifixion and resurrection, Christ went to the regions of darkness and proclaimed his victory over the devil and the demons. This belief spawned some very creative paintings by medieval and Renaissance artists. One painting shows a victorious Christ standing over the mouth of an enormous serpent, rescuing various Old Testament saints. This view offers one answer to the question, what happened to the Old Testament saints when they died? While we know that to be absent from the body is to be present with the Lord (2 Corinthians 5:8), it seems that Old Testament believers did not always have that assurance.

Some suggest that Christ liberated the righteous souls who were in the paradise part of Hades and thus "led captivity captive" (see Ephesians 4:8-10, KJV). The story of the rich man and Lazarus in Luke 16:19-31 seems to lend support for that view. If you ask me if this is true, I will have to say that I don't know. I think it's a plausible inference from various Bible passages, but we can't be certain.

Our problem is that we have a myopic view of the death of Christ, focusing on ourselves and what the cross means to us. But many passages suggest that the cross of Christ had a cosmic impact that touched the entire universe, from the highest heights to the lowest depths. Colossians 2:15 tells us that the cross of Christ conquered Satan and his demons.

The death of Christ brought startling changes in the spirit world, most of which remain hidden to us.

WHAT IT MUST MEAN

After surveying various possibilities and freely admitting there is much here about which we cannot be certain, this phrase indicates two bedrock truths that we can wholeheartedly embrace.

Christ Fully Experienced Death

This is the primary meaning of "he descended into hell." He knows what death is all about because he has been there. He entered the house of death, and he came out victorious (Revelation 1:18). Dr. W. A. Criswell said in a sermon he preached on Revelation 1:18:

> When they nailed his feet to the tree, and when they nailed his hands to the wood, and when he entered into the dark gloom of the grave, there did he trample down forever the kingdom of death. And when he arose triumphant from it, he carried death as a captive chained to his chariot wheels.[17]

I like that picture—death chained to the chariot wheels of Jesus. Our Lord could not have conquered death unless he fully entered into every dark part of the kingdom of death. And he did just that!

Christ Fully Defeated the Devil

Here are five ways the cross of Christ defeated the devil:

- His head was crushed (Genesis 3:15).
- His works were destroyed (1 John 3:8).
- His power was broken (Hebrews 2:14).
- His demons were disarmed (Colossians 2:15).
- His doom was guaranteed (John 16:11).

All this happened at the cross when God struck the mighty blow that left Satan defeated, disarmed, and disgraced. That's why we like to say, "It's Friday, but Sunday's coming!" I love the story of Charles Spurgeon, the great London preacher of the late 1800s, who awoke one night because he felt his bed shaking. Thinking it was caused by a thunderstorm, he looked outside but saw no clouds in the sky. "I woke up and looked, and there was Satan standing at the foot of my bed. Satan himself was shaking my bed. I looked at him and said, 'Oh, it's only you,' and rolled over and went back to sleep."

What should this truth mean to us?

We need not fear death.

Death is like a dark room that frightens us because we don't know what's in there. But the Creed tells us that Jesus has gone into every dark room ahead of us and tells us, "Come on in. I am here, and it is safe."

Death is like a dark room that frightens us because we don't know what's in there. But Jesus has gone into every dark room ahead of us.

An old hymn by Richard Baxter reminds us:

Christ leads us through no darker room
Than he went through before.
He that unto God's kingdom comes,
Must enter by this door.

We will all die sooner or later, but Christ has transformed death for the believer.

He has taken the sting out of death so that when we die, we do not cease living. When we stop living on this earth, we immediately begin to live in the presence of our Lord in heaven.

The work of salvation is absolutely complete.

Because Christ died for us and took our punishment, we cannot go to hell. Let me say that in a stronger way.

It is utterly impossible for a true child of God to go to hell.

Our Lord descended into hell so that we would never go there. He took the curse for us so the curse would never fall on us. "There is therefore no condemnation for those who are in Christ Jesus" (Romans 8:1).

The devil cannot ultimately defeat us.

Though he has great power and roams the earth like a roaring lion (1 Peter 5:8), and though he makes great pretensions and may at times fill us with dread, Satan's power has been broken once and for all. Hear the words of Martin Luther: "Through Christ hell has been torn to pieces and the devil's kingdom and power utterly destroyed . . . so that it should no longer harm or overwhelm us." All the enemies of Christ have been defeated. We know how the story ends. Jesus wins, and we win with him!

We will let Martin Luther have the final word on this subject:

And though this world, with devils filled, should threaten to undo us,
We will not fear, for God hath willed his truth to triumph through us.
The prince of darkness grim, we tremble not for him;
His rage we can endure, for lo! his doom is sure;
One little word shall fell him.

What is that "one little word" that brings the devil down? It is the name Jesus. On the cross Jesus Christ utterly defeated Satan, and he proved it by rising from the dead.

On that first Easter Sunday morning the word came down from heaven to the devil and all his demons: "Turn out the lights—the party's over." Do you feel defeated? Stand and fight. Do you feel discouraged? Stand and fight. Have you been tempted to give in? Stand and fight. Are you wavering between right and wrong? Stand and fight. Remember, the Captain of our Salvation has already won the battle. Satan can harass you, but he cannot destroy you. His doom is sure; one little word shall fell him.

THINK ABOUT IT!

1. What are some of the things that the phrase "He descended into hell" does *not* mean? What is the significance of each?

2. What does the Creed mean by this phrase? What is the significance of this? To you personally?

3. What did Jesus' death accomplish for us? What did it mean regarding the devil's war against God and against us? Have you personally received the forgiveness that Christ won for you through his death on the cross? If not, why not receive him as your Savior right now?

11

Going All In: "The Third Day He Arose Again from the Dead"

Christ has been raised from the dead, the firstfruits of those who have fallen asleep.

1 CORINTHIANS 15:20

Billy Graham once told *Time* magazine, "If I were an enemy of Christianity, I would aim right at the Resurrection, because that is the heart of Christianity." The founder of the Jesus Seminar, Dr. Robert Funk, offers a perfect example of what Billy Graham was talking about. This is how Dr. Funk explains what happened to Jesus' body after his crucifixion: "The tales of entombment and resurrection were latter-day wishful thinking. Instead, Jesus' corpse went the way of all abandoned criminals' bodies: it was probably barely covered with dirt, vulnerable to the wild dogs that roamed the wasteland of the execution grounds." When Thomas Jefferson wrote his version of the life of Christ, he removed all mention of the supernatural, including the miracles of Christ, the Virgin Birth, and the Resurrection.[18]

What would happen to your faith if tomorrow morning *USA Today* carried the headline, "Body of Jesus Found near Jerusalem"? Would it matter at all, or would you go on as if nothing had happened?

On this point the Apostles' Creed offers an unambiguous affirmation: "The third day he arose again from the dead." No ifs, ands, or buts about it. Jesus died on Friday; on Sunday morning he came back from the dead.

Credo

WHAT DOES IT MEAN?

When we say that Jesus rose from the dead on the third day, we mean that Jesus truly died on Friday afternoon, and on Sunday morning he personally, bodily, physically, literally rose from the dead, never to die again. He rose *personally*—it was Jesus himself, not some substitute. He rose *bodily*, meaning that it was his crucified body that was raised from the dead. He rose *physically*, meaning that he wasn't a ghost or a figment of someone's imagination. To say that he rose *literally* means that it really happened. And the word *resurrection* means that he was raised immortal and incorruptible, never to die again.

Jesus, having once experienced death and having triumphed over it, would never die again. He was raised immortal—alive from the dead—and he still lives today.

Jesus truly died on Friday afternoon, and on Sunday morning he personally, bodily, physically, literally rose from the dead, never to die again.

Why does this matter? First, *this is what the Bible teaches; so to deny it is to deny God's Word.* Everything in the Gospel records, everything in the book of Acts, everything in the epistles stands in perfect harmony on this point: Jesus died and then rose from the dead.

Second, *this is what really happened.* If you had been there that Sunday morning, you would have seen the empty tomb. If you had been with the disciples, you would have seen Jesus alive from the dead. Like Thomas, you could have checked out the evidence for yourself.

Third, *this is what the church has always believed.* The resurrection of Christ has always been a fundamental truth of Christian doctrine. If you truly do not believe in the resurrection of Jesus, you have placed yourself outside the boundaries of orthodox Christianity and are not a Christian at all—and you shouldn't be treated as one even if you happen to be a pastor or a seminary professor.

Fourth, *this is what the church's proclaims.* Read the book of Acts.

Study the sermons of Peter and Paul. The climax was not merely "Christ is crucified," but "Christ is risen from the dead!" That was the message that turned the world upside down. *The Son of God had come back from the dead!* Nothing like that had ever happened before. Jesus was crucified once and for all, but he did not stay dead.

WHAT IF IT DIDN'T HAPPEN?

In the early church some believers became confused because of a false belief that their loved ones who had died would not be raised from the dead. Paul addresses this problem in 1 Corinthians 15 by reminding his readers that the resurrection of believers depends on whether or not Jesus himself rose from the dead. When we stand at the graveside of a loved one, it's not unusual to wonder if we will ever see that person again. No one we know in this life has ever come back from the dead. It is noteworthy that in his opening response (vv. 3-11), Paul does not rebuke the Corinthians for their fears and doubts, nor does he try to prove the resurrection of the dead in some detailed argument. He points these erring believers back to the empty tomb and says, "Remember that God raised his Son. Everything hinges on that." Then for a few verses (vv. 12-19) he argues the contrary case: What if Jesus has not been raised from the dead? Four conclusions follow.

Our Faith Is Futile

He says this explicitly in verse 17: "And if Christ has not been raised, your faith is futile and you are still in your sins." The word *futile* means "useless, empty, vain, of no value." The Christian faith without the Resurrection is an exercise in futility. When Billy Graham was just beginning to rise to prominence in the 1940s, another young evangelist became well-known at the same time. Many people thought he was an even better preacher than Billy Graham. Charles Templeton and Billy Graham spoke together at Youth for Christ rallies across America and Great Britain. Templeton was gifted, brilliant, articulate, and a powerful preacher of the gospel. But in the years following World War

II, Templeton and Graham began to move in different directions. Templeton began to question many aspects of his Christian faith.

The Christian faith without the Resurrection is an exercise in futility.

Templeton attended a liberal seminary, pastored in Canada for a few years, and eventually gave up his Christian faith altogether. Later he became the host of a late-night talk show that made him the "Johnny Carson of Canada." In his later years he attacked the evangelical faith he had once preached. At one point he published a novel called *Act of God* that was built on the premise that the bones of Jesus had been discovered in the Holy Land, but the Catholic Church covered up the story because the leaders knew it would destroy Christianity.[19]

Toward the end of his life (he died several years ago), Templeton was interviewed by Lee Strobel for his book *The Case for Faith*.[20] The interview clearly shows that despite some regret, Templeton never gave up his skeptical unbelief. I mention his story because I wish to give Charles Templeton due credit, especially for his novel. He understood exactly what the apostle Paul was saying. If Christ is not risen from the dead, then the Christian faith collapses like a deck of cards.

We Are Still in Our Sins

This also is in verse 17. Christ's death cannot save us if he is still in the tomb. Not long ago I heard a man pray, "Lord Jesus, even if you didn't rise from the dead, at least we know our sins are forgiven." But that's the exact opposite of what Paul says.

We Will Never See Our Loved Ones Again

"Then those also who have fallen asleep in Christ have perished" (v. 18). Death has won the final battle if Christ did not rise, and our worst fears are realized as we lay our loved ones to rest—we will never see them again.

We Should Be Pitied

"If in this life only we have hoped in Christ, we are of all people most to be pitied" (v. 19). Sometimes well-meaning people say something like, "Even if Christianity isn't true, it's still the best way to live." The proper theological term for that is *baloney*. I don't want to spend my days following some clever fable. Life is too short to do anything but find the truth and then commit yourself to it 100 percent. If Jesus did not rise on the third day, then the "Hallelujah Chorus" is just another piece of nice music. If Jesus did not rise, then our prayers are empty, our preaching is in vain, our missionary work is useless, and the church stands for something that is not true. If Jesus is still in the grave, then we're just talking nonsense on Easter Sunday morning. That's what Paul meant—and he's right!

It all hangs on that little word "if." If Jesus did not rise . . .

But what if he did?

WHAT DIFFERENCE DOES IT MAKE?

Having stated the negative, Paul now triumphantly asserts the positive truth in verse 20: "But in fact Christ has been raised from the dead, the firstfruits of those who have fallen asleep."

We can simply reverse all of Paul's previous points. Now that Christ is risen . . .

- Our faith has meaning.
- We have forgiveness.
- We will see our loved ones who died in Christ.
- We can be certain about our own future.

What wonderful news this is. Now there is hope for the hopeless. Now light shines from heaven in the midst of the darkest corners of the world. Whatever your sin might be, no matter where you've been or what you've done, the blood of Jesus Christ can forgive you and wash you clean in one great moment of transformation. Heaven now becomes real, and death has lost its victory. We still die, but we don't stay dead forever. There is good news from the graveyard because Jesus has come back from the dead.

(Jesus said) **"I am the resurrection and the life ... Do you believe this?"** This is a ... question which makes sense only during an all-night vigil or in the stillness of smoke-filled waiting rooms. A question that makes sense when all of our props, crutches, and costumes are taken away. For then we must face ourselves as we really are: rudderless humans tailspinning toward disaster. And we are forced to see him for what he claims to be: our only hope. (Max Lucado, God Came Near)

"Do You Ever Doubt?"

Not long ago the twentysomething singles group at the church I pastor invited me to an "Ask Pastor Ray" night. That's always fun because the group is lively, and they pepper me with unpredictable questions. That night fifty to sixty of us sat in a big circle in our church dining room. I told them I would be glad to answer questions on the Bible, the Christian life, or theological issues, or they could ask about my personal life. No topic is off-limits. Near the end of the evening, a young lady raised her hand and asked, "Pastor Ray, when I listen to you speak, you always sound so certain about everything. Do you ever doubt?" I told her I thought that was a very important question.

I know that when I preach or when I write, I do sound very certain. Part of that is intentional. For one thing, I know what I believe, and I'm not shy about presenting my views in a forceful manner. Also, when a man stands up to preach, he should preach his faith, not his doubts. People have enough troubles of their own without me adding to their burden. But having said that, I think the question deserves an answer.

Yes, I do have doubts. I don't talk about them very much, but I doubt every day. (After I preached a sermon on this, one of the elders of the church was concerned about that statement—did I really mean it? Absolutely, I said. I have doubts and questions that come to my mind every single day.) I don't know how a person could be a Christian and not have doubts from time to time. Faith requires doubt in order to be faith. If you ever arrive at a place where all your doubts are gone, you will know that you are in heaven.

Faith requires doubt in order to be faith. If you ever arrive at a place where all your doubts are gone, you will know that you are in heaven.

When I answered the question that night, I mentioned that just that afternoon I had spoken at a funeral service for a good friend. I have done more funerals than I can remember. The hardest part for me is driving away from the grave. The finality of leaving someone in the ground weighs on my soul.

Now I know that to be absent from the body is to be present with the Lord (2 Corinthians 5:8). But I believe that by faith. What I see with my eyes is a man being buried in the ground. Over the years I've seen all the death I care to see, even though I will likely see much more before my time on earth is done. Everyone I've ever buried is still in the grave. I'm waiting for my first resurrection.

Where will we find hope in the face of death?

Going "All In"

I shared an illustration with the singles that surprised them and made them laugh. Sometimes when I'm flipping through the TV channels, I'll stop and watch poker tournaments. You might not think poker would be exciting, but it works well on TV because it's an amazing study in strategy and the intricacies of human behavior. In every game of high-stakes poker, there comes a defining moment that separates the winners from the losers. At that moment a player says two words—"All in." He thinks he has the best hand; so he takes his chips and pushes them to the middle of the table. He flips his cards over so everyone can see them, and then he stands up. Going "all in" means you are risking everything on one hand. If you win, you win it all. If you lose, you lose it all. You can't win a tournament unless you're willing to go "all in" at some point.

Credo

As a Christian and as a pastor, I confess that I do have my doubts. I know that people put their trust in what I say, and that weighs on my heart. I wonder sometimes if all the things I say about life and death, about God and salvation and heaven and hell are really true. In the end I come back to this: A long time ago I decided to go "all in" on the resurrection of Jesus Christ. I risked it all on Jesus' rising from the dead on the third day. I've taken my stand at the empty tomb, and I'm not ashamed to stand with Christians across the centuries and say, "I believe that Jesus Christ rose from the dead."

I invite you to do the same. If he did rise from the dead, we're going to be okay. We can have our doubts and our worries and fears, and as we drive away from a funeral we can have many unanswered questions. But that's not what matters. Our faith is not determined by our doubts. Our faith rests on what happened in a garden tomb outside Jerusalem more than two thousand years ago. If Jesus rose from the dead, we're on the winning side. Death has had a field day for a long time. I've staked my entire future and all I believe on the truth that Jesus lives today because he conquered death on the first Easter Sunday morning.

Thanks be to God for the empty tomb. As much as I marvel at the Virgin Birth of Jesus, as much as I wonder at his sinless life, as much as I glory in the cross of Jesus, it is the resurrection of Jesus that makes Christianity unique among all of the world religions. Doubt if you will, but the tomb is still empty because he is not there. He is risen, just as he said. You can bring your doubts to the empty tomb, but you have to make a choice. You can't stay on the fence forever.

You can bring your doubts to the empty tomb, but you have to make a choice. You can't stay on the fence forever.

Doubting is not a sin, but at some point you have to stop doubting and start believing. Either you believe or you don't. I've made up my mind. I'm going "all in" on the resurrection of Jesus because on "the third day he arose again from the dead."

THINK ABOUT IT!

1. How would your life—your needs, your spiritual standing, your goal and hopes—be different if Jesus hadn't truly risen from the dead?

2. What has the resurrection of Jesus done for you? What does it mean to you personally?

3. What does it mean to go "all in" for Jesus? Have you done this? When, and under what circumstances? Share your experience with someone else today. Or if you haven't yet taken this step, why not today?

12

A Friend in High Places: "He Ascended into Heaven and Sits at the Right Hand of God the Father Almighty"

Since then we have a great high priest who has passed through the heavens, Jesus, the Son of God, let us hold fast our confession. . . . Let us then with confidence draw near to the throne of grace, that we may receive mercy and find grace to help in time of need.

HEBREWS 4:14, 16

This is one of the most remarkable statements in the Apostles' Creed, and it is also one of the most neglected areas of Christian doctrine. Even though we believe in the ascension of Christ, we tend not to think about it very much, at least when compared to the death and resurrection of our Lord. We know that Jesus died for our sins and rose from the dead for our salvation, and we know that we couldn't be saved without Good Friday or Easter Sunday. But where does the Ascension fit in? To many people it seems like a PS to the gospel—perhaps merely a convenient way for Christ to get back to heaven. But is it essential to our Christian faith?

We face certain difficulties when we consider the ascension of our Lord. The event itself is only briefly mentioned in Mark, Luke, and Acts (and is not cited at all in Matthew and only minimally in John). By contrast both the crucifixion and the resurrection are described by all four Gospel writers in detail. And it is difficult for us to visualize exactly what happened. Yet it is rare to find someone who doubts the ascension of Christ.

But a quick glance at church history tells us there is more here than meets the eye. For one thing, every major Christian creed includes the ascension of Christ. We find it in the Apostles' Creed, the Nicene Creed, and the Athanasian Creed. The liturgical calendar always includes Ascension Day—always on a Thursday, always forty days after Easter. And both the event and the doctrine behind it are highly biblical. In writing this chapter, I came to a fresh appreciation of how many times the New Testament writers mention the Ascension and its consequences. Here are just a few examples:

Then he led them out as far as Bethany, and lifting up his hands he blessed them. While he blessed them, he parted from them and was carried up into heaven. And they worshiped him and returned to Jerusalem with great joy. (Luke 24:50-52)

And when he had said these things, as they were looking on, he was lifted up, and a cloud took him out of their sight. (Acts 1:9)

No one has ascended into heaven except he who descended from heaven, the Son of Man. (John 3:13)

He who descended is the one who also ascended far above all the heavens, that he might fill all things. (Ephesians 4:10)

He was manifested in the flesh, vindicated by the Spirit, seen by angels, proclaimed among the nations, believed on in the world, taken up in glory. (1 Timothy 3:16)

We have a great high priest who has passed through the heavens, Jesus, the Son of God. (Hebrews 4:14)

. . . Jesus Christ, who has gone into heaven and is at the right hand of God, with angels, authorities, and powers having been subjected to him. (1 Peter 3:21-22)

The Creed gives as much space to the ascension as it does to the cross and to the Resurrection.

Many other verses also speak of Christ's exaltation at the Father's right hand in heaven and what this truth means for believers. I find it striking that the Creed gives as much space to the Ascension as it does to the cross and to the Resurrection, evidence that the earliest Christians believed that the Ascension stood on an equal basis with the events of Good Friday and Easter. The truth of Christ's ascension answers three important questions:

- What happened to Jesus?
- Where did he go?
- What is he doing now?

HE ASCENDED INTO HEAVEN

We can state what we know about the event itself in very simple terms. While Jesus is speaking to his disciples in Bethany (several miles east of Jerusalem), he blesses them and is taken up into heaven before their eyes.

They were there, they saw it, it really happened.

It was not a figment of their imagination or a dream or a vision. Unlike the Resurrection, which no one saw as it was happening, the disciples actually saw Jesus ascend into heaven. Both Luke and Acts say that Jesus was "taken up " (NIV) into heaven. The verb has the idea of being lifted straight up into the air. Note that he ascended bodily—not as a spirit, but in his glorified body, the same body that was crucified, the same body that was raised incorruptible.

I emphasize this point because in recent years liberal scholars have attacked the ascension of Christ as scientifically impossible. People don't just float off the earth and disappear into thin air, they object. The story sounds like Captain Kirk on the TV series *Star Trek*: "Beam me up, Scotty." Critics suggest that the ascension stories represent a pre-scientific view of the universe that no one takes literally today. To them, the Ascension is not a literal event but a parable that teaches us that Christ is now in heaven.

The Ascension is no harder to believe than the Resurrection.

Of course, those same liberal scholars don't believe Jesus rose from the dead either. When you make science your god, the miracles of the Bible go out the window and instead of believing the Bible, you stand in judgment over it.[21]

Let me simply point out that if God can raise his Son from the dead, he can certainly take him back home to heaven. It comes down to a simple question: Am I willing to believe that God can do what he said he would do? The Ascension poses no problems for people who believe in the God of the Bible.

By means of the Ascension, Jesus' triumphant return to heaven signaled that the days of his suffering were over at last. No more crown of thorns. No more vicious insults. No more beatings. No more cruel scourging. No more crowds screaming for his blood. No more betrayal. No more mocking. Now no one spits in his face. Never again will nails be driven through his hands or his feet. Never again will a spear be thrust into his side. Never again will he cry out, "My God, my God, why have you forsaken me?" Never again will his mother weep as he dies. Never again will his dead body be taken down from a cross. Never again will he be prepared for burial. Never again will he spend a night in the tomb. Death and the grave are behind him forever. Put away the whip, the hammer, the nails; fold up the linen cloth. He who suffered more than any man will suffer no more.

THE UNLIMITED CHRIST

But there is more to consider. Because Jesus has returned to heaven, he is now liberated from all time and space limitations. Have you ever wished you could spend some time with Jesus face to face? In trying moments I feel that if I could see him, I would be stronger. If only I could see him, my struggles would vanish. I suppose all of us have thoughts like that from time to time.

It's not wrong to feel that way. There is a longing in every redeemed heart to see Jesus up close and personal. And yet Jesus said, "It is to your advantage that I go away " (John 16:7). How can that be? As long as Jesus stayed on earth, he was bound by the limitations of time and space. If he was in Atlanta, he couldn't be in Berlin. But now that he has gone back to heaven and has sent us the Holy Spirit, he is with us all the time. "I am with you always, to the end of the age" (Matthew 28:20).

Come what may, the saints are preserved in Christ Jesus, and because he lives, they shall live also. (Charles Haddon Spurgeon, SPURGEON'S DAILY TREASURE FROM THE PSALMS)

How good to know that our Lord will never leave us. When we stumble, he is with us. When we feel his presence, he is there. When we think he has left us, he is there. When we doubt him, he is there. When we forget him, he is there. When we give in to temptation, he is there. Jesus is always with us. But that is true only because he ascended to heaven.

HE SITS AT THE FATHER'S RIGHT HAND

The New Testament uses three words to describe Jesus' status in heaven:

- He is *exalted.*
- He is *glorified.*
- He is *enthroned.*

In the ancient world when a king wished to honor someone, he offered him a seat at his right hand. That seat was the greatest honor and the supreme glory the king could confer on anyone. What does it mean to say that our Lord is now seated at the Heavenly Father's right hand? First, it means *he has a permanent place in heaven.* When he returned in triumph, our Lord didn't have to search for a seat in heaven, and that seat at the Father's right hand is his forever.

Second, *it means that his work of redemption is now complete.* While he was on the earth, he spoke often of "the work" of the Father (for example, John 4:34; 9:4; 17:4). His work came to a climax when he hung on the cross, bearing the sins of the world (2 Corinthians 5:21).

When Jesus died, God poured out his wrath on the Son, even though Jesus was perfect and pure and wholly innocent.

As our sinless substitute, he took the punishment we should have received so that we might go free. Just before he died, Christ shouted out, "It is finished" (John 19:30), which literally means "paid in full." I can never be charged with the guilt of my sins because Jesus paid it all. The Ascension signifies that the Father has accepted the work of his Son.

> I can never be charged with the guilt of my sins because Jesus paid it all.

Hebrews 10:11 reminds us that there were no chairs in the tabernacle. The priests stood to perform their work because their work was never done. Every day the priest would kill more animals, signifying that the price of sin had not yet been paid. But when Christ returned to heaven, he sat down because he had offered himself as the one sacrifice for sin forever (v. 12).

Third, it means *he is now in the place of supreme and highest honor in the universe.*

God has exalted him and given him a name that is above every name.

We learn from Philippians 2:9-11 that someday every knee will bow to the name of Jesus and every tongue will confess that Jesus Christ is Lord, to the glory of God the Father. Consider what this means:

• The victim has become the victor.

- The crown of thorns has been replaced by the crown of eternal glory.
- The spear has been replaced with the scepter of regal authority.

By seating his Son at his right hand, the Father vindicated his Son. Now at last Jesus receives what he truly deserves—glory, laud, and honor. Philippians 2:5-7 tells us that Christ "made himself nothing," emptying himself of the outward trappings of deity in order to take on the form of a man. He humbled himself by leaving the palaces of heaven to be born in a stable in Bethlehem. He veiled his glory and lived a life of humiliation. All of us feel it was unfair for the King of kings to be treated so rudely by those he came to save. As he hung on the cross, onlookers jeered as his life ebbed away. They laughed at his pain and cried, "If you are the Son of God, come down from the cross" (Matthew 27:40). The Ascension means that Jesus has been vindicated in all that he came to do, and his days of humiliation are over forever. In 1871 Frances Ridley Havergal wrote an ascension hymn called "Golden Harps Are Sounding, " proclaiming this truth:

> Golden harps are sounding, angels voices ring,
> Pearly gates are opened, opened for the King:
> Christ the King of glory, Jesus, King of love,
> Is gone up in triumph to his throne above.

> He who came to save us, he who bled and died,
> Now is crowned with glory at His Father's side.
> Nevermore to suffer, nevermore to die,
> Jesus, King of glory, is gone up on high.

> Praying for his children in that blessed place,
> Calling them to glory, sending them his grace;
> His bright home preparing, faithful ones, for you;
> Jesus ever liveth, ever loveth, too.

> All his work is ended, joyfully we sing;
> Jesus hath ascended: glory to our King!

HE INTERCEDES FOR THE SAINTS

This is where the truth of Christ's ascension touches everyday life. First, *because he lived on the earth and endured deep suffering, he knows what we are going through*. A friend recently told me, "I have learned I can trust Jesus even though he knows all about me." Think about that for a moment. He knows you through and through. He knows where you were last night, what you did, and what you thought about doing. He knows all about every dumb thing you've said and done and thought in the last week—and he still loves you. That's good news.

Second, because he is now in heaven, he intercedes for us with the Father. The word *intercede* means "to speak up on behalf of someone else." Christ is now in heaven praying for us. What a marvelous thought this is—and what a balm for troubled souls. When I am down in the dumps, Jesus prays for me. When I falter under the load, Jesus prays for me. When my faith gives way, Jesus prays for me. When I fight a losing battle against temptation, Jesus prays for me. There's even more than that. Often when I am asked to pray for someone, I can't seem to find the appropriate words, and I feel as if my prayers are in vain. But Jesus in heaven comes alongside me, takes my pitiful prayers, and transforms them into powerful petitions before the throne of God, as does the Holy Spirit (Romans 8:26-27). When I can't pray, when the words won't come, Jesus prays for me.

> Jesus in heaven comes alongside me, takes my pitiful prayers, and transforms them into powerful petitions before the throne of God. When I can't pray, when the words won't come, Jesus prays for me.

Hebrews 7:24-25 adds the encouraging thought that because Jesus lives forever, he intercedes forever, which is why we are saved forever. In Old Testament times the priests kept dying. The good ones died, and the bad ones died. Just about the time you got used to a certain high priest, he died, and another man took his place.

But since Jesus lives forever, we can be certain that he never stops praying for us. And because he never stops praying for us, he saves us completely—to the very end.

OUR MAN IN HEAVEN

Hebrews 4:14-16 calls Christ a great high priest who has gone into heaven. Because he walked on earth, he knows what we are going through and is able to sympathize with us in our struggles. Because he is now in heaven, he can help us in all our troubles. When we go to the throne of grace, we don't have to worry about being turned away because Christ himself is there and has grace to help us in time of need.

We have a Friend in high places—in fact, in the highest place in the universe.

Think of it this way. When you're in trouble, you need two things: someone who cares about your problems, and someone who can help you out. If your friend cares but isn't in a position to help you, you'll get sympathy but no concrete help. If your friend could help you but doesn't care about your problem, well, that's like not having a friend at all. What you need is someone who cares and is in a position to make things happen for you. That's what Jesus is—a Friend in high places who loves to come to the aid of his people.

First John 2:2 adds the encouraging truth that Christ is our attorney in heaven, our advocate who speaks to the Father in our defense. When the devil comes and makes a claim against us, Jesus speaks up on our behalf and pleads his own blood in our defense. The Father looks at the Son, sees his pierced hands, and says, "Case dismissed." Let me tell you the best part of this truth: Jesus has never lost a case yet. Because Jesus has been exalted to the right hand of God the Father, he's in the place of highest authority in the universe, and he's speaking on our behalf all the time.

Jesus is our 24-7 advocate in heaven—twenty-four hours a day, seven days a week. Acts 7 shows us how this works. When Stephen preached his bold sermon before the Jewish Sanhedrin (the Supreme Court of Israel), he recited the history of the nation, showing how the Jews had consistently rejected God's messengers. He told them they had murdered God's righteous Son (v. 52)! The rulers didn't like that kind of talk, so they gnashed their teeth at him. But Stephen cried out, "I see the heaven opened, and the Son of Man standing at the right hand of God" (v. 56).

What does this mean? On earth Stephen stands before a corrupt human court, but in heaven there is another Judge. And this Judge will also be the attorney for the defense. In Roman courtrooms, the judges stood to announce the verdict. As Stephen is dying, Jesus stands to announce heaven's verdict: "They can kill you on earth, but I will defend you in heaven." The world cries out, "Guilty!" But Jesus says, "You are my child. My blood covers your sins. You are welcome in heaven forever."

When Jesus ascended into heaven, he took his glorified humanity with him.

The physical body of Christ is now in heaven, which means that someday when we are raised from the dead, we won't be raised as spirits but as real people with our physical bodies glorified just like Jesus'. He not only redeemed our souls—he also redeemed our bodies. If we are in Christ, we have his promise that our flesh will be renewed and gloriously raised in the resurrection. Then we shall see him as he is, and we will be with him forever.

The Ascension guarantees our Christian destiny.

Because he was raised, we too will be raised. Because he ascended, we too will ascend. Because he is in heaven, we will join him there someday. I recently spent six days speaking at the Word of Life Bible Conference Center in Hudson, Florida. After my final message, an older couple drove me to the Tampa airport so I could catch my flight back to Chicago. As we talked, the father shared a tragic story about the death of one of his sons at the age of thirty-three. It happened just as the son was completing his training to be a missionary. Cancer took his life only three months after diagnosis. Before he died, he encouraged his parents with the words, "Don't worry about me. I'm just being transferred to Headquarters." His parents have cherished those words ever since their son died.

Where does that kind of faith come from? What hope do any of us have of going to heaven? Surely it is this:

We will be where he is, and we know where he is because he ascended into heaven.

At the moment of death the children of God can rest assured that the Christ who ascended bodily into heaven will take them to be with him and will one day raise their bodies immortal and incorruptible (1 Corinthians 15:52-53).

THE TUG OF HEAVEN

Because of the Ascension, we may rest assured that the religion of Christ is true.

God has accepted Jesus Christ, and because God accepted him, he will accept all those who trust in him. Because he is safe in heaven, we will someday be safe in heaven. We will be where he now is. The Ascension shows us how we should spend our life—looking up. A little boy went outside on a windy spring day to fly his new kite. As the wind blew, the kite flew higher and higher until it finally disappeared from view in the clouds far above. After a few minutes a bystander asked, "How do you know the kite is still attached?" "I can feel it tugging on the string," the boy replied. The same is true for us today. Christ is pulling us away from the earth toward our eternal home. We may not see him with our eyes, but we feel his tug in our hearts. We know where he is, and we know that where he is, we will someday be.

Every day Jesus tugs on our hearts, pulling us up toward heaven so that when we finally get there we won't feel like strangers. One day soon the Lord will give us one final tug, and we'll end up in heaven forever. Until then, let the people of God rejoice—Christ has conquered! He has won the victory and has defeated every foe. This is what we mean when we say, "He ascended into heaven and sits at the right hand of God the Father Almighty."

THINK ABOUT IT!

1. Why do we give so much attention to the death and resurrection of Jesus but so little to his ascension? Do you agree that the Ascension plays a major role in the Christian faith? Why or why not?

2. What is the significance of Jesus' *sitting* at the Father's right hand—not only theologically, but personally?

3. What do the biblical statements about Jesus praying for you mean to you? In what ways does this encourage or strengthen you or give you hope?

13

Here Comes the Judge: "He Shall Come to Judge the Living and the Dead"

"Let not your hearts be troubled. Believe in God; believe also in me. In my Father's house are many rooms. If it were not so, would I have told you that I go to prepare a place for you? And if I go and prepare a place for you, I will come again and will take you to myself, that where I am you may be also."

JOHN 14:1-3

You never know where you will find spiritual truth. Not long ago I received a letter from Mary Jo Lynch, who thirty-five years ago lived with her husband Dudley in my hometown of Russellville, Alabama. Dudley Lynch pastored Cumberland Presbyterian Church, built near a strip mine on State Highway 24 between Russellville and Belgreen. It was a typical, tiny, country, brick church.

Dudley worked a variety of second jobs to support his family. At one point he opened up a sandwich shop and sold the greasiest hamburger in America—the Lynchburger. I remember sitting at the counter talking about the Bible while Dudley filled the orders. That was the beginning of my knowledge of Bible doctrine. I never saw him without a smile on his face.

Dudley died in 1992. Mary Jo wrote a letter shortly afterward. I didn't hear from her again until recently. She is now in her seventies and living near Lexington, Kentucky. She wrote me because while browsing through her church library she found one of my books. So she wrote to say hello. At the end she added these thoughts:

> With whatever discernment I have at this point in my life, it seems to me that these are the best of times and the worst of times. The best of times, because God's true church is alive and well and the Spirit is using some unexpected ways to get the attention of the lost people all around us. Who would ever have thought that Mel Gibson would make a movie that would cause so many to either dust off the Bible they have, or buy one and read the biblical account of the crucifixion?
>
> It is the worst of times because never in the history of our country has the stability of the family, especially marriage, been threatened as it is now. It is my hope and prayer that there will be a movement back to Christian values and to an acknowledgment of God in society in general. But maybe it is too late for that. I just get this feeling that God is pouring out his grace upon us in these last days before he will pour out his wrath in the Tribulation period. He is not willing that any should perish but all come to repentance.

The best of times, the worst of times, the last days, the Tribulation, and God is not willing that any should perish. Amen.

IT IS THE BEST OF TIMES

Thanks to Mel Gibson's film *The Passion of The Christ*, for a brief period Jesus became popular in America. Consider too the incredible success of Rick Warren's book *The Purpose-Driven Life*, and several years ago the popularity of *The Prayer of Jabez* by Bruce Wilkinson, and the amazing run of the Left Behind series by Tim LaHaye and Jerry Jenkins. Even the commercial success of Dan Brown's *The Da Vinci Code* (a book that attacks Christianity) points to the spiritual hunger (and spiritual confusion) of this generation.

David Brooks, senior editor of the *Weekly Standard*, recently wrote

On Paradise Drive, an analysis of modern culture. He draws this conclusion: "We work harder than any other people on the face of the earth. What on earth are we looking for? And I think the answer is that we're looking for heaven. We're looking for paradise."[22] But no matter how hard we try, we cannot find the happiness we seek.

No matter how hard we try, we cannot find the happiness we seek.

Not long ago I received an e-mail from a young man who had read one of my books.

I had a rough beginning in life and I always had a hard time with prayer and in faith, I was raised a Catholic but I don't know where I stand. I am starved for faith and I envy those who have it, deep down inside I long for God to be a part of my life. Today I made a testimonial to change my lifestyle and be the person I was meant to be. Out of despair I went to the local bookstore in search of some guidance. I came across your book and I decided to buy it. I never heard of you or had a clue where your church was until about an hour ago. I don't know if this is a coincidence but I live in downtown Oak Park and I just thought it was a little weird that I randomly pulled a book out of the Christian section at Borders and it happened to be a local [author]. Every day of my life has been a battle, I am finally enjoying some success with my career but I have been spiritually empty. . . . I am ready to accept God and his will into my life; I have been spiritually deprived for too long. I pray that this incident is to bring me closer to God; today was the first day that I prayed with passion in a long, long time. Thanks to finding your book I am making an effort to walk towards God. Thank you for your time and I appreciate your prayers.

His words reminded me of Ecclesiastes 3:11, which says that God has put eternity inside every heart. We were made to know God, to love him, and to serve him. In the words of Augustine, "O Lord, our hearts were made for you, and we will not find rest until we find rest in you."

IT IS THE WORST OF TIMES

It is not difficult to find evidence on the negative side of the ledger. One obvious example is the attack on marriage and the family in the form of so-called "gay marriage." Those who support it are acting on their presuppositions. Gay marriage is simply the latest manifestation of humanity in full-throttle rebellion against its Creator. My greater concern is with the people inside the church who ought to know better. Christians ought to be leading the fight for moral values in our society. Too many of us have been silent for too long.

Or consider Internet pornography. A woman whose family has been torn apart because a family member became addicted to pornography on the Web begged me to warn people about the danger. We can add abortion—the legalized destruction of the unborn—to the list as well. Then there is the growing deep divide between those who believe in moral absolutes and those who don't.

Certainly we can also add the rise of radical Islam and the Age of Terror that has engulfed us all since 9/11. Recently Marlene drove me to O'Hare Airport so I could catch a flight to New York. As we approached O'Hare, I spotted a thick, black cloud coming from the vicinity of the airport. What was my first thought? *Terrorists have struck the airport.* Before 9/11 that would have seemed farfetched. But now the veneer of security has been ripped away. The Madrid and London mass transit bombings have affirmed our fears.

Related to that is the prevailing theological confusion over salvation: Is Jesus really the only way to heaven? I once heard Erwin Lutzer predict that this would be the dominant issue of the early twenty-first century. Events since then have proved him correct. Praying in Jesus' name has been banned at many public gatherings. Now we are told that Muslims, Christians, and Jews all worship the same God, and those who say Jesus is the only way are called bigots.

As a result of all these factors, we are an angry, nervous nation. Our usual self-assurance has been replaced by critical impatience. Not that long ago if you paused for a second when the traffic light turned green, people waited patiently. Now they hit the horn and almost immediately hit it again. We get angry more quickly, and sometimes *really* angry. I confess that I see this change in myself as well.

The precise date of the Second Advent has been designedly withheld from us in order that we should maintain our attitude of watchfulness and that we remain on the very tiptoe of expectation. (Arthur W. Pink, THE REDEEMER'S RETURN)

All that brings us to this phrase from the Apostles' Creed: "I believe . . . he shall come to judge the living and the dead." These simple words consist of two complementary truths:

- Jesus is coming again.
- Jesus is coming again to judge the living and the dead.

One of every thirteen verses in the New Testament deals with some aspect of our Lord's return to the earth.

The New Testament refers to the Second Coming of Christ in over three hundred verses. That means one of every thirteen verses deals with some aspect of our Lord's return to the earth. It is so central to the New Testament that Christians everywhere have always believed that Jesus will return someday. Though we differ (and argue!) over the details, Christians of all varieties unite in believing that Christ himself will return to the earth. Jesus said in John 14:3, "I will come again." His second coming will be

- *personal* (it will be Jesus and not some substitute).
- *literal* (not a vision or a dream).
- *visible* ("Every eye will see him," Revelation 1:7).
- *sudden* (not a gradual return).
- *unexpected* ("like a thief in the night," 1 Thessalonians 5:2).

Acts 1:11 makes it clear that Jesus *himself* will one day return to the earth. The same Jesus who left will one day return. He will come back personally, and his coming will be sudden and unexpected. Luke 24:50-52 informs us that as Jesus reached out his hands to bless his disciples, he began to rise from the face of the earth, evidently without any warning whatsoever. We can assume that his return to the earth will be no less astonishing and no less surprising.

The actual, historical figure who lived two thousand years ago on the other side of the world will return to the earth.

That future event—the literal, visible, bodily return of Christ to the earth—will be more marvelous, more startling, and more spiritually dynamic than anything that has happened in the last two thousand years. No event may seem less likely to modern men and women, and yet no event is more certain in the light of inspired Scripture.

KEEP YOUR EYES ON THE MIDDLE EAST

Where are we on God's timetable? I offer two simple answers. On one hand, *no one knows the day or the hour of Christ's return*, and it is dangerous to be overly dogmatic regarding the signs of the times. On the other hand, *the Bible gives a detailed picture of the events surrounding the Second Coming*. God has revealed to us the general picture of world events in the days leading up to Christ's return. One thing I can say is, keep your eyes on the Middle East. That's where the story started, and that's where it will come to an end. The final great act of human history will take place not in Tokyo, New York, or London but in Jerusalem and in the nations surrounding Israel. Are we living in the last days? No one knows for sure. But consider these facts:

- The Bible lays out a clear pattern of events concerning the last days. If you put together the various strands of prophetic teaching from the Old and New Testaments, you will see a fairly detailed picture of the end-time landscape—morally, politically, spiritually, militarily, and economically.
- There is an amazing similarity between our world and the world the Bible describes at the end of time. Take your Bible in one

hand and the newspaper in the other, and it won't take you long to see how well they fit together.

- If that is true, then we may indeed be the generation privileged to see the coming of Jesus Christ.
- Every sign points in one direction—it won't be long now.

A WORD FROM PETER

But before we sell our houses or cars and move to the mountains to await the Lord's return, as some misguided souls have done in the past, let us heed the words of 2 Peter 3:3-10. In this passage Peter addresses a puzzling question, one that bothered believers in the first century and troubles thoughtful people today: why hasn't the Lord returned already? What is he waiting for? Does the two-thousand-year delay mean that he isn't coming at all? Listen to Peter's answer:

> *Knowing this first of all, that scoffers will come in the last days with scoffing, following their own sinful desires. They will say, "Where is the promise of his coming? For ever since the fathers fell asleep, all things are continuing as they were from the beginning of creation." For they deliberately overlook this fact, that the heavens existed long ago, and the earth was formed out of water and through water by the word of God, and that by means of these the world that then existed was deluged with water and perished. But by the same word the heavens and earth that now exist are stored up for fire, being kept until the day of judgment and destruction of the ungodly. But do not overlook this one fact, beloved, that with the Lord one day is as a thousand years, and a thousand years as one day. The Lord is not slow to fulfill his promise as some count slowness, but is patient toward you, not wishing that any should perish, but that all should reach repentance. But the day of the Lord will come like a thief, and then the heavens will pass away with a roar, and the heavenly bodies will be burned up and dissolved, and the earth and the works that are done on it will be exposed.*

This passage is full of important truth that deserves close consideration.

Credo

Despite What the Scoffers Think,
the Second Coming Is Certain
Because God Promised It

Scoffers say, "Twenty centuries have come and gone, and still Jesus has not come. Give it up. He's not coming back." To which Peter replies, "Think about Noah's flood." Before the Flood, men lived in reckless disregard for God. They sinned in every way possible. But one day the skies poured forth water, and the fountains of the great were opened, and water covered the entire earth. If God judged the world once, he can do it again—only this time the coming of Christ will bring a judgment of fire to the earth.

The Second Coming Will Usher in a
Day of Judgment for the Ungodly

Notice the sequence of words: "water . . . fire . . . judgment . . . destruction." God destroyed the world once with water; the next time he will destroy it with fire. For the ungodly, the Second Coming of Christ will be bad news indeed.

The Second Coming Is Delayed
to Give People a Chance
to Come to Christ

Here is the good news. The delay the scoffers talk about is actually God's gift to them.

He purposely delays the Lord's return in order to give men and women more time to repent.

Verse 9 reveals God's tender heart toward the lost. He does not enjoy sending people to hell. Contrary to popular opinion, he is not some crazed old man in a white beard, laughing while he hurls lightning bolts to the earth. For more than two thousand years he has held back final judgment in order to give rebellious men and women a chance to surrender to Jesus Christ.

For more than two thousand years God has held back final judgment in order to give rebellious men and women a chance to surrender to Jesus Christ.

As the Creed says, Christ will eventually judge "the living and the dead." All must stand before him and give an account. Not long ago I talked with a retired military man who had served his nation in dangerous places around the globe. He made a surprising comment. "Our soldiers are ready to fight anyone, anywhere. But our basic problem is different. We're afraid to die." He didn't mean our soldiers (many of whom have already made the supreme sacrifice). He was talking about America as a nation.

We're afraid to die because we are so prosperous that this world has become like heaven to us.

We love our wealth so much that we can't bear to let it go.

TERRY PLATT

But death comes to all of us sooner or later, and it comes to some of us sooner than we expect. When my friend Terry Platt was diagnosed with leukemia, he knew he had a rough battle ahead of him. He endured three extremely difficult rounds of chemotherapy, each causing intense sickness of varying kinds. He was in the hospital for the fourth round (of eight) when he died. His work with Gospel Light often took him out of town, but whenever he was in Oak Park on Sunday, he and his wife, Barb, would be in the same pew, the last one in the middle section, on the east side, near the door. Often I would stop and chat with him between services.

Terry always had a joke and a story, and there was always a smile on his face. As my wife, Marlene, and I walked into a Christmas Eve service, we spotted Terry and Barb. "I thought I heard your voice," he said with a chuckle, then turned serious and said, "The doctors tell me I have less than a year to live."

Many times during his chemotherapy the pain was excruciating.

But he never complained. He would tell his oncologist, "I'd like to stay alive as long as I can because I'm going to be in heaven for a long, long time." When the doctor asked him how he knew he was going to heaven, Terry laughed and said, "Now you're in my territory," then proceeded to share his faith in Christ.

A Personal Version of John 14:6

Knowing that he was in the hospital, I called Terry one Easter morning from my office at church, just before the first service. His voice was weak when he answered the phone, but when he realized it was me he immediately said, "He is risen! He is risen indeed!" He was full of faith and hope in the Lord. Before we hung up, Terry shared with me his own personal translation of John 14:6, based on his study of the Greek text. Later he wrote me a note that turned out to be his final e-mail to me:

> April 24, 2004
> Good Morning Ray,
> I am home from the hospital for a few days. Can't believe the year is 1/3 over. I was so blessed weeks ago when I attended church. Along with your sermon I thought you might like the expanded version of John 14:6. This is a personal translation from Greek studies when [I was] in Bible College.
> "Jesus Christ Himself said, I am the way, and that is to say the only way, I am truth, and that is to say the only truth, and I am life, and that is to say the only life. It is absolutely impossible for anyone to go where the Father is unless they go through me." That makes it pretty clear!

Thank God, there is no chemotherapy in heaven, no cancer, and no hospitals. There are no graveyards dug into the hillsides of heaven. For Terry, the worst is over. The bright sun of eternity now shines in his face, and somewhere up there he is telling stories, laughing, singing, praising. If he could, he would say to all of us, "Don't worry about me. I'm fine. I'll see you soon."

IS THERE ANY HOPE?

I agree with Mary Jo Lynch. These are the best of times, and these are the worst of times. And I think the situation for believers will get simultaneously better and worse as we march toward the climax of human history. Let me say plainly that I don't know when Jesus will return. I don't know, and I won't set a date. I hope he comes soon. He might come today. I do know this:

Jesus will return when everything is ready in God's plan. Not a moment earlier, not a second later.

How close are we to that great day when the trumpet will sound, the dead in Christ will rise, and we will be caught up together with them to meet the Lord in the air? Perhaps very close. Certainly closer than we think.

For those who know Jesus Christ, there is enormous hope. If he comes today, we win. If he comes in fifty years, we win. If he comes in a thousand years, we win. These are great days to be alive, the greatest days in all of human history. Think of it—we may well be the generation privileged to see the return of Jesus Christ. If this really is the terminal generation, the smartest thing you can do is to give your life 100 percent to Jesus Christ. Trust him completely, so that if he comes today or tomorrow or next week or in a hundred years, you will have no regrets but will be ready to see him when he returns.

THINK ABOUT IT!

1. Is it the best of times and the worst of times? In what way(s)? What does this have to do with your life?

2. What is your response to the fact that Jesus will return to earth to judge the living and the dead? What does this mean to you?

3. Why is Jesus Christ waiting so long before returning to earth? Do passages like 1 Thessalonians 4 and 2 Peter 3 ring true to you? What is your personal response to what they say? Are you ready to face God's judgment, whenever it occurs for you? Why or why not?

14

When God Comes Near: "I Believe in the Holy Spirit"

On the last day of the feast, the great day, Jesus stood up and cried out, "If anyone thirsts, let him come to me and drink. Whoever believes in me, as the Scripture has said, 'Out of his heart will flow rivers of living water.'" Now this he said about the Spirit, whom those who believed in him were to receive, for as yet the Spirit had not been given, because Jesus was not yet glorified.

JOHN 7:37-39

This is a moment of high drama. It is the last day, the greatest day, of the final feast of the year, the Feast of Tabernacles. It usually took place in early October, at the time of the final harvest, and it was a great celebration. For seven days the Jews lived in lean-to tents or booths made of palm branches, leaves, and tree limbs. This was their way of remembering the forty years that their ancestors spent wandering in the wilderness. That was a hard time, a long time. A whole generation died while waiting to enter the Promised Land.

Why celebrate that difficult period? Because every day God provided manna and quail. Though they lived in the desert with the sand and heat and flies and desolation all around them, God never failed them. God prepared a table in the wilderness and fed them for forty years. So the Jews came to Jerusalem for seven days each year, made their lean-tos, and celebrated God's goodness.

But God not only gave them food in the wilderness—he also gave them water. When the people accused Moses of bringing them into the desert to die of thirst, the Lord told Moses to take the same staff he'd used to part the Red Sea and hit the rock. He did, and water gushed out, more than enough for all the people. It was a mighty miracle. The people had grumbled against God, and he provided for them anyway.

During the Feast of Tabernacles, the priest would go to the Pool of Siloam. There he filled a golden urn with water and brought it back to the Temple. While he poured the water on the western side of the massive altar, a choir of four thousand singers accompanied by 287 instrumentalists sang, and the people sang Psalm 118: "Oh give thanks to the LORD, for he is good; for his steadfast love endures forever!" The priest repeated that ritual every day for seven days, and the people cheered for joy each time. The eighth day was the final feast day of the entire year. On that day there was a solemn convocation, but the priest did not go to the Pool of Siloam to draw water.

On that day—the greatest day of the final feast—the day with no water—Jesus stood up and spoke to the throngs of people crowding the Temple precincts. The fact that he stood would have gotten their attention since Jewish rabbis normally sat when they taught. On the one day when there was no water, Jesus said, "If anyone thirsts, let him come to me and drink." The Jews understood him immediately. For Jesus to say those words at that moment meant, "I am the rock that brought forth water in the wilderness. Come to me, believe on me, and I will give you living water from heaven."

His words still offer a message of hope to a thirsty world.

WE COME TO CHRIST BECAUSE WE ARE THIRSTY

If we are thirsty, we go to the refrigerator and get some water or milk or iced tea or a can of pop. Or we go to the faucet and turn it on, and if we don't turn it off, water pours out twenty-four hours a day. Most of us rarely experience true thirst. We know that a man can live for weeks without food, but he can only live a few days without water.

Once thirst takes over, it becomes a raging demon. When thirst controls you, you will do anything, anything at all, to get a few drops, even lie or cheat or steal.

Inside all of us is a thirst that nothing in this world can satisfy.

We all have a God-shaped vacuum that only he can fill. Some people thirst for sexual fulfillment and hop from one relationship to another. Some people move from job to job. Some leave their spouses for someone else, but they're still not happy. Adrenaline junkies are always looking for the next adventure, the next battle to fight, trying to fulfill the wild-at-heart impulse inside. Some people thirst for significance, others for power, others for fame or wealth to fill the lonely void inside.

We come to Christ because we are thirsty, and until we see our need and cry out to him for help, we will never come at all.

As Jesus said, only the sick need a physician, only the hungry will be fed, only the lost are found, only the thirsty drink the living water.

WHEN WE COME TO CHRIST, OUR THIRST IS QUENCHED

How simple it is to be saved. It's like drinking a glass of cool water on a hot day. Notice the verbs that Jesus uses: "Come . . . drink . . . believe." Jesus used simple words so everyone could understand the Good News.

How simple it is to be saved. It's like drinking a glass of cool water on a hot day.

Not long ago I received a letter from a prisoner in Kansas named Bennie. He had received a copy of my book *An Anchor for the Soul*. Here is his letter exactly as he wrote it:

Hello Pastor Ray,

First of all, may God bless you. I pray that this letter finds you in the best of health. Me, I'm blessed, Sir, I just got done reading your book, and believe me, I have been a mess up all my life, and my wife and my kids have always be saved, "Godly people." It's always been

me the messed up father and husband, but after reading your book—
Oh, I'm in prison now for drugs and I got to do 58 months, but after
I read your book, I asked the Lord Jesus into my life, and I don't
know what happen, but I do know it were good. So thank you for
everything and I would like for you to assist me more about knowing Christ.

Pastor Ray, I would really like to hear from you.

Thank you.

Bennie

Those are the words of a man who has found living water; he just
doesn't know how to explain it yet.

Another e-mail I recently received came from a man who has been
attending the church I pastor for a few months.

Pastor Ray,

I am writing to you today to share with you how Calvary changed
my life. Almost two years ago for unknown reasons I decided to
check out Calvary one Sunday morning. I liked what I saw and heard
and began to attend pretty regularly.

Then sometime last fall something happened in my life that was
profoundly different. I believe that is when I developed a personal
relationship with Jesus Christ. All of a sudden material things don't
matter very much and I have an inner peace that I have never had
before.

The rest is history. I began to come every Sunday and because of
your encouragement at the membership seminar I joined an ABF
where I have made new friends and learned many new things. I can't
explain how all this happened but I am very thankful that it did.

"I can't explain how all this happened." That sounds a lot like what
Bennie said—"I don't know what happen, but I do know it were good."
In a real sense it doesn't matter whether you're in prison or on the outside because apart from Christ we're all in the same boat. We're all hungry and thirsty and desperately searching for something we can't quite
find. Then one day we meet Jesus, and suddenly everything is different.

Here is one mark of true conversion: we are deeply changed by Jesus, and we know it.

That's the meaning of, "Out of his heart will flow rivers of living water." The Greek literally reads "out of his belly," meaning out of the deepest place, the seat of the emotions. When we talk about a belly laugh, we mean the same thing. A belly laugh comes from deep within us. The deep change Jesus makes touches us at the very core of who we are.

You will know you are converted when you come to Jesus and something happens to you that you cannot fully explain.

True conversion is more than walking an aisle, saying a prayer, or raising a hand. True conversion means that Almighty God enters your life and takes up residence deep within. You can truly say, "I am converted" when you know that God has done something for you that only God can do. True conversion goes beyond religion, which is why religious people who depend on their own good works are often the last to be converted. Such religious people go to church and go through the motions, they may even pray the prayers and say all the right words, but they have a Sahara heart—hot, parched, barren, empty.

> Religious people go to church and go through the motions, they may even pray the prayers and say all the right words, but they have a Sahara heart—hot, parched, barren, empty.

But when Jesus comes in, living waters flow out. And they keep on flowing.

WHEN OUR THIRST IS QUENCHED, LIVING WATER FLOWS FROM US TO OTHERS

Living water flows from God into us, and then from deep within us the river flows out from us for the benefit of others. The concept of a river of living water can be found in various places in the Old Testament, including Isaiah 44:3, "For I will pour water on the thirsty land, and streams on the dry ground; I will pour my Spirit upon your offspring, and my blessing on your descendants." In John 7:39 Jesus tells us that this living water is the Holy Spirit. That's the connection with the Apostles' Creed, which says, "I believe in the Holy Spirit." The Holy Spirit brings God to us. When Jesus was on the earth, his name was Immanuel—God with us. Now that he has gone back to heaven, the Holy Spirit comes and brings God to us. The moment we believe in Jesus, the Holy Spirit opens the springs of life, and a river of living water begins to flow from within us.

This spring [of God's grace] is inexhaustible, it is full of grace and truth from God, it never loses anything, no matter how much we draw, but remains an infinite fountain of all grace and truth; the more you draw from it, the more abundantly it gives of the water that springs into eternal life . . . just as a learned man is able to make a thousand others learned, and the more he gives, the more he has—so is Christ, our Lord, an infinite source of all grace, so that if the whole world would draw enough grace and truth from it to make the world all angels, yet it would not lose a drop; the fountain always runs over, full of grace. (Martin Luther)

God never gives his blessings simply to be hoarded. He gives his blessings to us so we can share them.

The Holy Spirit brings God to us so we can bring God to others.

A genuine believer in Christ is not self-centered. He says, "I have been greatly blessed. I must pass what God has done for me along to others. I can't keep it all for myself." What God gives us, we must give away. If it's money, it's not ours anyway. If it's our time, it all belongs to God anyway. If it's something we own, we can give it away because we don't really own anything—God owns it all. If it's a helping hand, we can do that because God reached down and helped us.

THE GREATER GOLDEN RULE

Behind this principle is the truth I call the Greater Golden Rule: "Do unto others as God has done unto you." Has God showered you with love? Then love others. Has God been kind to you? Then be kind to others. Has God shown grace (undeserved favor) to you? Then show grace to others. Has God forgiven you? Then forgive others. Be a river of living water for some thirsty soul this week. Note that the word "rivers" in John 7:38 is plural. Many rivers of living water will flow out from us. Think of the Nile plus the Danube plus the Amazon plus the Mississippi plus the Ganges plus every other great river in the world— inexhaustible abundance.

Do unto others as God has done unto you.

We need the Holy Spirit today as never before. The early Protestant Reformers adopted this motto: "Reformed, yet always reforming." No church ever truly arrives. We are always on a journey with the Lord. Every church has faults and flaws and weaknesses. Every church is in continual need of further reformation by the Holy Spirit. Nearly twenty years ago I heard J. Vernon McGee speak at a commencement service at Dallas Theological Seminary. He was in his eighties at the time. Several years later he went home to be with the Lord. I have forgotten everything he said that day except for one statement. He commented that if he could start his ministry over again as a young man, he would do one thing differently—he would preach more about the Holy Spirit because that is the great need of the church.

We need the Holy Spirit to come to us in a new way because there is always more of God to experience. In Ephesians 3:19 Paul prayed that his readers might be "filled with all the fullness of God." The word "filled" has the idea of being dominated by something. If you are filled with rage, rage will dominate your life. If you are filled with love, love controls your life. If you are filled with joy, joy permeates your life. And when you are filled with God, God himself will dominate your life. This pictures the total transformation of your personality by virtue of the presence of God in your life.

Don't shy away from the implications of this truth. God desires to pour his life into ours and to fill us until we're full. This prayer will never be completely answered in this life. In eternity we will continue to experience more and more of "the fullness of God," and we will never come to the end of who he is.

It is the work of the Holy Spirit to bring us continually into a deeper, more profound experience of who God is. He brings more of God to us as we gladly open our hearts to him.

THINK ABOUT IT!

1. What types of thirst do you experience in your life day to day? Has Christ placed rivers of living water within you? If so, how did this come about? If not, do you want him to do this for you?

2. Is the living water that Jesus put within you flowing from you to others? If so, in what ways? If not, why not?

3. What do you think Paul meant when he prayed that the Christians in Ephesus would be "filled with all the fullness of God"?

15

God Has a Big Family: "The Holy Catholic Church"

[Jesus said,] "I will build my church, and the gates of hell shall not prevail against it."

MATTHEW 16:18

The Apostles' Creed says, "I believe in . . . the holy catholic church." Now, not everyone agrees with the Creed. People say, "I believe in God, but I don't believe in the church." "I'm spiritual, but I'm not religious, so I don't go to church." "The church is full of hypocrites." "I can worship God on the golf course." "I believe in my own way. I don't need to go to church and have someone tell me what to believe."

Some people (especially non-Roman Catholics) have a problem with this part of the Apostles' Creed. They stumble over the "c" word ("catholic") because it makes them feel vaguely uncomfortable, as if they are saying something they shouldn't say. When I preached on the Apostles' Creed to my congregation, I received more comments on this phrase than on any other. Why do we say this phrase, and what does it mean?

The word *church* refers to those who have been called out of the world by God to join together as followers of Jesus Christ.

The word *church* refers to those who have been called out of the world by God to join together as followers of Jesus Christ.

157

Credo

Now, the church is not a building. I pastor a church that meets in an historic sanctuary built in 1901 for the First Presbyterian Church of Oak Park, Illinois. But no matter how lovely it is, the building is not the church and can never be the church. Although it is built of stone, the stones are dead, and the church that Jesus is building is made of "*living* stones" (1 Peter 2:5). The word *church* in the New Testament never refers to a building. It always refers to people.

So what is meant by the phrase in the Apostles' Creed, "I believe in . . . the holy catholic church"? Up until this point, everything in the Creed has been either invisible or distantly historical. When the Creed mentions "God, the Father Almighty," we understand that we cannot see him with our eyes. The same goes for the Holy Spirit. When we speak of Jesus Christ, we proclaim our belief in a Person who last walked on the earth twenty centuries ago. But we make a sharp right turn when we say, "I believe in . . . the . . . church." (Forget the "holy catholic" part for a moment.) With these words the Creed plunges us deep into the nitty-gritty of life in the twenty-first century. Now we're being asked to affirm our faith in an institution that all too often seems unworthy of our trust.

The historical record is checkered at best. Men have often killed each other mercilessly in the name of Jesus Christ. In our day we have seen respected Christian leaders fall prey to immorality and greed. The sex abuse crisis in the Catholic priesthood has tarnished the church (I mean the church as an institution, not just the Roman Catholic Church) in the eyes of many people—believers and unbelievers alike. There was a day when society looked to churches to provide moral and spiritual leadership. That day (for better or worse) is long gone.

Perhaps you remember as a child folding your hands together, with your finger interlaced downward and saying, "Here is the church, here is the steeple. Open the door and see all the people." That's the problem and the challenge and the blessing and the hope of the church—the people. Inside every church you find

- contentious people,
- greedy people,
- unreasonable people,
- unkind people,
- thoughtless people,
- critical people,
- cantankerous people.

We're all sinners in need of God's grace. If we knew the naked truth about every other person in the church, and they knew the naked truth about us, we'd all run screaming from the sanctuary.

But if people are the problem, they are also the hope of the church.

Take away the people and there would be no church. The Creed challenges us to set aside our misconceptions and our frustrations and say, "I truly do believe in the church." We need to affirm that the church exists because of God, that this all-too-human institution that fails too often because it is full of fallible human beings is still worth believing in because of God. He started it, and it belongs to him. These are amazing and even countercultural assertions, but they are also entirely biblical.

With all its schisms and divisions, with all its weaknesses and obvious deficiencies, the church is that unique organism chosen by God to storm the very citadels of Satan and to prevail, to snatch the souls of men and women from the darkened bastions of death itself. (David L. Larsen, CARING FOR THE FLOCK)

I know that many people have become skeptical about the church. Some people have been deeply hurt by thoughtless and even cruel church members. But we must not let the foolish acts of others keep us from saying what Christians have said across the centuries: "I believe in the church."

Four key words have historically been used to describe the church, two of them come directly from the Apostles' Creed, the other two come from the Nicene Creed.

Credo

THE CHURCH IS ONE

First, the church is *one*. When Jesus said, "I will build my church," he used the singular, not the plural.

There is only one true ekklesia—the assembly of those who have been called out of the world to follow Christ.

The oneness of the church is the basis for true Christian unity. Paul explains the basis of our unity in Christ by using the word "one" seven times in Ephesians 4:4-6. "There is one body and one Spirit—just as you were called to the one hope that belongs to your call—one Lord, one faith, one baptism, one God and Father of all, who is over all and through all and in all."

The church is one because it is built on Jesus Christ: "For no one can lay a foundation other than that which is laid, which is Jesus Christ" (1 Corinthians 3:11). Samuel Stone said it well in his famous hymn:

> *The Church's one foundation*
> *Is Jesus Christ her Lord,*
> *She is his new creation*
> *By water and the Word.*
> *From heaven he came and sought her*
> *To be his holy bride;*
> *With his own blood he bought her,*
> *And for her life he died.*

> *Elect from every nation,*
> *Yet one o'er all the earth;*
> *Her charter of salvation*
> *One Lord, one faith, one birth;*
> *One holy name she blesses,*
> *Partakes one holy food,*
> *And to one hope she presses,*
> *With every grace endued.*

When Jesus prayed in John 17:21 that "they may all be one," he was asking the Father to help believers demonstrate on earth the perfect unity that exists in heaven between the Father and the Son. We are never told to create unity; God has already done that in Christ.

We are to "maintain" (Ephesians 4:3) the unity God has already created among all true believers.

This is a doctrine that is easier to talk about in theory than it is to work out in practice.

Catholic Joe

As I thought about the oneness of the church, Catholic Joe popped into my mind. His real name is Joe Nast, but on staff we call him Catholic Joe. Joe is an old and dear friend who has been around Calvary Memorial Church since the day I arrived. Joe is in his late seventies now or perhaps his early eighties (that's just a guess; he might be older than that), and his health is not good. But when he was able to get out and about, I would often come to church and find a packet of material Joe had collected on his visits to various churches.

The first time I met him he handed me a piece of paper with some questions written on it. The first one went something like this: "Jesus said, 'I will build my church.' But the Protestants are divided into twenty thousand different denominations and sects. How could they be the church Jesus was building when there is only one Roman Catholic Church?" Over the years we have had many discussions. We eventually became very good friends, and I learned a great deal about the Catholic Church from Joe's patient tutelage.

I have to confess that Joe's question stumped me when I first read it. Now that I'm older and a bit wiser (or at least more experienced), I think I would answer it this way: Though the Catholic Church seems like one church, it's really more like a huge umbrella that covers many groups and factions that in many cases have little to do with each other. You have the Mel Gibson, ultraconservative, Latin Mass Catholics on one end of the spectrum. On the other end you have Liberation Theologians. In many ways the Catholics seem as badly divided as the Protestants. Certainly there is a huge divide between conservative and liberal Catholics that amounts to a war for the heart and soul of their church.

But I don't want to leave the matter there. As Joe pointed out, Protestants are indeed divided into many groups. In response to those divisions, the mainline denominations have attempted to come together through the ecumenical movement. After forty years of talk, the movement has very little to show for itself. The major result has been to almost totally de-emphasize Bible doctrine. How else will you get Baptists and Lutherans and Episcopalians and Methodists to worship together in the same church? This de-emphasis on doctrine led to more and more people coming together who believe in less and less until everyone believes in nothing at all. You just keep stripping away the truth until virtually nothing is left. When everything is up for grabs, no one can tell right from wrong.

The Most Fragmented City in America

But that's not the end of the story either. I only mentioned the Catholics and the mainline Protestants so I could say something about the evangelicals—conservative, Bible-believing Christians. We have our own set of problems. We say we like to work together, and we say we believe in unity, and we say that we want to pray together, and we say it's a good thing when churches unite their resources to do something great for the Kingdom of God. But we say that sort of thing more often than we actually do it. We are divided racially, economically, ethnically, and geographically. Bringing the body of Christ together is a gargantuan task.

How should we view the oneness of the church in light of the enormous divisions in Christendom? The best way is to understand that despite our differences, we still have a great deal in common. We share a common faith in the Bible as the Word of God, in the doctrine of the Trinity, in the Virgin Birth, in the death of Christ for our sins, and in his resurrection from the dead. Noting the areas of common faith even while upholding secondary distinctive doctrines is not a compromise. We should be glad when we find others who share our faith at certain points, even as we insist on the great truth of justification by faith alone handed down to us from the Reformers, and ultimately from the New Testament.

So when we say the church is one, what church are we talking about? We mean the church in the New Testament sense—the assembly of those who have been called out of the world to follow Jesus Christ. Those who truly believe in him are truly members of the church, regardless of their denominational affiliation. We extend Christian fellowship to all true believers everywhere because we are fellow members of the family of God by faith in Jesus Christ. Not everyone who joins a church—any church—is born again. Some don't clearly understand the gospel. Others prefer a religion of good works instead of the gospel of grace. But the Lord knows his own sheep, and they hear his voice and follow him (John 10:27; 2 Timothy 2:19). He is building his church one person at a time as men and women begin to follow him. That church is the one church Jesus has been building for two thousand years.

> Those who truly believe in Christ are truly members of the church, regardless of their denominational affiliation. We extend Christian fellowship to all true believers everywhere because we are fellow members of the family of God by faith in Jesus Christ.

God has a big family, and if you know Jesus, if you have trusted him as your Lord and Savior, you are part of that family.

THE CHURCH IS HOLY

To say the church is holy can seem to mean "holier than thou." That the church has sometimes fallen far short of God's design cannot be disputed. And we all understand that Christians can sometimes be terribly hypocritical. But that's not the heart of the matter.

The word holy *means "set apart for God."*

Anything that belongs to God is holy by association with him. We call the Bible the Holy Bible because it comes from God. The church is holy because the people are holy, and the people in the church are holy because they belong to God by virtue of their redemption through the blood of Jesus Christ. First Peter 2:9 says that believers are "a chosen race, a royal priesthood, a holy nation, a people for [God's] own possession." Those four phrases describe who we are simply by virtue of God's grace, God's work in us. He saved us, and then he declared us his chosen people, a royal priesthood, and a holy nation. But that doesn't end the story. The verse also says God did this so that we may "proclaim the excellencies of him who called you out of darkness into his marvelous light." We, the holy people of God, are to live so that we bring glory to him.

> **The people in the church are holy because they belong to God by virtue of their redemption through the blood of Jesus Christ.**

To be holy means to go against the tide because the tide is running in the wrong direction. It means to swim upstream because the stream is flowing into the foul pit of destruction. Holiness always involves rejecting the ways of darkness and walking in the light of the Lord.

When the church is truly the church, it will be both salt and light in the world.

Remember that salt is both an irritant and a preservative. If the church never irritates the world, it isn't doing its job. G. K. Chesterton put it this way: "A dead thing can go with the stream, but only a living thing can go against it." God calls us to swim upstream every day, and then he gives us the strength to do it.

THE CHURCH IS CATHOLIC

Some evangelicals are troubled by the word "catholic" in the Creed because they think it has something to do with the Roman Catholic

Church. But catholic with a small *c* simply means "universal." When applied to the church, it means that the message of the gospel is for all people everywhere, in every generation and in every situation. We find this emphasis in many places in the New Testament. In Matthew 28:19 and Mark 16:15 Jesus instructs us to make disciples in every nation. Repentance and forgiveness of sins are to be preached in his name to all nations (Luke 24:47). We are to be witnesses to the ends of the earth (Acts 1:8). So, to be "catholic" means that we intend to preach the gospel by every means possible to reach as many people as possible in every place possible, so that by God's grace we can win as many people as possible to saving faith in our Lord Jesus Christ. The church is to be "catholic" or universal in its outreach.

But the church is to be "catholic" in its makeup as well.

We should expect and pray that our local congregations will in some small way reflect God's heart for the whole world.

In 1900, 80 percent of all Christians lived in North America and Europe. By 2000, things had shifted so dramatically that 60 percent of all Christians lived in South America, Africa, and Asia. By 2050, non-Latino whites will make up only 20 percent of the Christian church worldwide. There are four times more Presbyterians in Korea than in the U.S., and there are more Anglicans in Africa than in Great Britain. In Scotland only 10 percent of church members go to church on any given Sunday, while in the Philippines 70 percent of all church members go to church every week. In our generation we are seeing the Great Commission being fulfilled as a harvest of souls comes in from every tribe and nation and from every people group on earth.

THE CHURCH IS APOSTOLIC

To be apostolic means that the church follows the faith preached by the apostles of Jesus. Acts 2:42 says that on the Day of Pentecost, three thousand new believers devoted themselves to "the apostles' teaching."

It's not the apostles as men that we follow; we follow their doctrine.

A church is apostolic to the extent that it follows the teaching of

Credo

the apostles in the New Testament. All twenty-seven books are part of the "apostles' teaching" that forms the foundation of our faith. When the Bible speaks of "the faith that was once for all delivered to the saints" (Jude 3), it means that the true church adheres to the teaching laid down in the New Testament.

What, then, is the church? The church is the worldwide body of true believers in Jesus who go against the flow of society, whose faith is based on the Bible, and who preach the gospel to every nation.

J. I. Packer calls the church the "supernatural society of God's redeemed people." The church is not an organization like the Rotary Club or the Woodland Hills Flower Society. What does this mean for us? Here are a few implications for us to consider.

We Are Part of Something Big—Much Bigger Than Us

If we grasp even a tiny part of what God wants to do through the church, we will be cured forever of small vision and selfish churchianity. Sometimes I can get so tied up (or bogged down) in the details of church life that it can seem like my church is all that matters. But seen properly, it is but one tiny outpost in the great army of God that stretches around the world.

My church is but one tiny outpost in the great army of God that stretches around the world.

We Need Each Other

Fire is a symbol of God's work in the world. When the Spirit comes in, he sets our hearts afire for the Lord. Even the brightest flame goes out eventually. But when the burning timbers are piled together, the flame grows brighter and brighter.

God never intended you to live the Christian life alone.

We were made to live together in unity with our brothers and sisters in the church—not only in the church universal but in the local church that you attend on Sunday. Can you grow spiritually without the church? For a while perhaps, but not for a lifetime, and not in the way God intended. We need each other for friendship, fellowship, discipleship, prayer, encouragement, support, worship, united outreach, and, when necessary, correction and redirection.

We Need a Worldwide Focus

The church is called to go into all the world and preach the gospel, and no local church can do it alone. A truly "catholic" church has a heart for the nations of the world. Not long ago I ran across a church with a wonderful name—The Church of All Nations. What a truly beautiful, biblical, soul-stirring concept—a church with intentional focus on the nations of the world. In a deep sense, every church should be a church of all nations.

We Need the Church, and the Church Needs Us

We are better and stronger when we find our place in the church, and the church is better and stronger when we are there. We sometimes speak of the church as a "fellowship of faith" and as a "community of believers." But there can be no fellowship unless the fellows show up and meet together. And there can be no community unless we intentionally decide to commune with each other. The early church father Cyprian said, "He who has God for his father has the church for his mother." That statement contains great truth.

It is through the church and in the church and by the church that the gospel comes to the world.

The church is the place where we learn and grow by rubbing shoulders with other believers and thereby learn to become devoted followers of Christ.

Dietrich Bonhoeffer said that the church is the place where our dreams are shattered, and that is a good thing. New believers often enter the church expecting to find a little bit of heaven on earth. We all hope and expect that our brothers and sisters in Christ will treat us better than the people of the world. And we all have certain ideas about music and worship and preaching and what the church should do and how it should go forward. But sooner or later we discover that the saints are not always saintly and that the people of God are not always godly. Sometimes they can be cantankerous and unkind. The local church routinely disappoints us.

> **It is only in the nitty-gritty of life together with all its disappointments and rude awakenings that we discover the Holy Spirit at work in us.**

Once our false expectations are shattered on the hard rocks of reality, then (and only then) do we begin to experience the grace of God. It is only in the nitty-gritty of life together with all its disappointments and rude awakenings that we discover the Holy Spirit at work in us. In the church we are thrown together with some people with whom we'd never otherwise associate. And that's a good thing because God uses others to shape us into the image of Christ.

I'M A CHURCHMAN

As I come to the end of this chapter, I gladly reaffirm that I still believe in the church. I've seen the good, and I've seen the bad. When the church is good, it is very good. When the church is bad, it can be very bad indeed. But through it all I still believe in God's church. Though it is weak, fallible, and in need of much improvement, it still remains the best hope of the world. Think of a world without Christian missionaries, Christian hospitals, sanitariums, rest homes, Christian relief agencies. What if there were no Christian schools, colleges, or universities? Imagine a world without the Bible or Christian music or the saving message of the gospel. As bad as the world is today, it would be immeasurably worse without the church of Jesus Christ.

We cannot turn away from the church just because it is imperfect. If we turn away from the church, we turn away from Jesus himself because the church is the body of Christ on earth.

Jesus said, "I will build my church, and the gates of hell shall not prevail against it" (Matthew 16:18). It doesn't always seem that way. The church is divided and weak, but it will prevail. Its leaders often fail, but the church will prevail. Sometimes the services are dull, but the church will prevail.

The church will prevail, not because of anything we say or do, but simply because Jesus said so. Individual churches wax and wane, pastors come and go, some churches fall prey to false doctrine, and leaders disappoint us. But God's church will prevail. Jesus said it, and his Word will not be broken.

In light of all this, what should we do?

- Pray for the church!
- Love the church!
- Join the church!
- Serve in the church!
- Support the church!
- Get involved in the church!
- Make it better by being part of it!
- Don't be a spectator—join the team!

Why care about the church? Jesus is there. That ought to be reason enough.

THINK ABOUT IT!

1. The church is one. What does this mean? What does it not mean? So why are there so many different religions and denominations? Is this good or bad?

2. The church is holy. What does holy mean? If the church is holy, why is there so much moral failure by spiritual leaders?

3. The church is catholic (universal). What does this mean? What does this not mean? In what specific ways is the church to be universal? What is your role in this?

16

All One Body We: "The Communion of Saints"

You have come to Mount Zion . . . and to the assembly of the firstborn who are enrolled in heaven.

HEBREWS 12:22-23

The Apostles' Creed says, "I believe in . . . the communion of saints." Because these words come near the end of the Creed, we may tend to overlook them, but we shouldn't because they teach us something important about the Christian church. In preparing this chapter, I was interested to discover that the phrase "the communion of saints" was a late addition to the Apostles' Creed. It was added several centuries after "the holy catholic church." It's worth pondering exactly what this phrase was supposed to add that wasn't already covered. Then a friend gave me a key to understanding both phrases. He put it this way:

> The Holy Catholic Church teaches us that the church *spans the globe.*
>
> The Communion of Saints teaches us that the church *transcends time.*

The word "communion" translates the Greek word *koinonia.* That's a very common word in the New Testament, meaning fellowship or partnership. It means to share together in a close relationship. In secular Greek it was used for a marriage, a business partnership, a community, or a nation bound together by common goals. Preeminently the word applies to friendship. Acts 2:42 uses this word to describe the intimate closeness of the early Christians who lived together, ate their meals together, and shared all things in common.

The word "saints" simply means "holy ones." In the New Testament *saint* is a synonym for *Christian* or *believer*. The apostle Paul used the word *saints* in several of his letters to describe all believers. He wrote to the saints in Rome and to the saints in Corinth and to the saints in Ephesus and to the saints in Philippi. To many of us *saint* refers to an extraordinary Christian, but the New Testament never uses the word that way.

I preach once a year at the Word of Life Conference Center in Hudson, Florida. For the last few years the same man has either picked us up or taken us back to the airport. I can't remember his name, but I can never forget him because he always greets me the same way: "Hello, saint!" He greets everyone that way. And he is entirely biblical in his use of the term because we are all saints of God. It is perfectly proper to speak of Saint Jane or Saint Jeff or Saint Jose or Saint Don or Saint Fred. If you know Jesus, you are a true saint of God.

Our fellowship ought to be as wide as the whole body of Christ.

To say that we believe in the communion of saints means that we believe there is an intimate connection between all true believers in Jesus.

Everyone who belongs to Jesus belongs to me, and I belong to them.

I draw a simple conclusion from this: Our fellowship ought to be as wide as the whole body of Christ. In the last few years God has expanded my own horizons in this area. I have discovered to my delight that God has his people scattered in some very unusual places, and I have learned there are many different ways to worship God in spirit and in truth. I learned to do a little worship dance at the YWAM base in Belize. Along with my friend John Sergey I observed a Greek Orthodox liturgy in St. Petersburg, Russia. I clapped and cheered with enthusiastic Haitian believers during an evangelistic campaign. I have preached in an evangelical church on the banks of the Volga River and joined in worship with the King of Kings church, a messianic, charismatic congregation that meets at the YMCA in Jerusalem. When we visited Jos, Nigeria, a few years ago, the church we attended took a special offering for the building fund. They called people to come forward by groups and put their offerings in a big metal tub in the front of the church. So while we all stood and clapped and sang, the different groups came forward singing and dancing, bringing their offerings with them. When the time came for the church leaders to come forward, I went with them, dancing as I went forward with my offering. To be honest, my dancing wasn't much more than shuffling my feet, and I wasn't very good at that, but I did it, and I enjoyed it. God has continually pulled me out of my comfort zone in the last few years to show me that his family is much bigger than I ever imagined.

THE GOSPEL IS FOR EVERYONE

Romans 1:16 is very helpful in this regard: "For I am not ashamed of the gospel, for it is the power of God for salvation to everyone who believes, to the Jew first and also to the Greek." The last phrase introduces the universal dimension of the gospel. The Jews were God's chosen people on earth. Although most of the Jews have not become followers of Christ, the gospel still has the power to save them if they will only believe. "Greek" means Gentile, that is, non-Jew. The gospel of Jesus has the power to build a bridge over the chasms of race, education, age, social status, skin color, family background, language, culture, and all the other things that divide the human race. Sometimes we are tempted to soften the gospel in order to broaden our fellowship, but the reverse is closer to the truth. When we are firm on the gospel, we will have joyful fellowship with God's people from many different backgrounds.

The gospel of Jesus has the power to build a bridge over the chasms of race, education, age, social status, skin color, family background, language, culture, and all the other things that divide the human race.

WE HAVE COMMUNION WITH CHRIST

We see this clearly in 1 John 1:1-4:

That which was from the beginning, which we have heard, which we have seen with our eyes, which we looked upon and have touched with our hands, concerning the word of life—the life was made manifest, and we have seen it, and testify to it and proclaim to you the eternal life, which was with the Father and was made manifest to us—that which we have seen and heard we proclaim also to you, so that you too may have fellowship with us; and indeed our fellowship is with the Father and with his Son Jesus Christ. And we are writing these things so that our joy may be complete.

We can never be in communion with others until we are in true communion with God. (Martyn Lloyd-Jones, FELLOWSHIP WITH GOD)

Everything we do is based on this truth. We have fellowship with God through his Son, Jesus Christ. And only in Christ do we have fellowship with one another. What sets us apart from the Rotary Club or a country club is that we have fellowship with God. The church is a fellowship of men and women who have a personal relationship with Jesus Christ.

WE HAVE COMMUNION WITH THE SAINTS ON EARTH

Back to 1 John 1 for a moment. In verse 7 he adds an important dimension to what he has already said: "But if we walk in the light, as he is in the light, we have fellowship with one another, and the blood of Jesus his Son cleanses us from all sin." I take it that "one another" refers both to God and to other believers.

Walking in the light allows us to have fellowship both with God and with other believers.

Because God is light and we are the children of light, when we walk in that light we are where God is and where his children are. We're no longer alone in the darkness of sin and rebellion. Once we begin to grasp this, all our relationships will be radically changed. We may be sinners, but we are sinners saved by God's grace. That changes how we treat our spouse and our children, the way we relate to our friends and relatives. Once we understand what God has done for us, we realize, "It's not about me. It's about reaching out to other people in Jesus' name."

WE HAVE COMMUNION WITH THE SAINTS IN HEAVEN

Hebrews 12:1 speaks of this when it says we are surrounded by a great "cloud of witnesses." Imagine that you are high up in Olympic Stadium in Athens, Greece, looking down on the athletes as they compete for Olympic gold. Some are throwing the javelin, others the shot put. Over there a man gets ready for the pole vault; a few feet away a group of runners stretch in preparation for the marathon. The stands are crowded with spectators from many nations cheering for their athletes. Hebrews 12:1 pictures the saints on earth in the arena while the saints in the heavenly grandstands cheer them on. Looking around, you see James and John. Over there is Paul, and you see Peter and Mark not far away. As you continue looking, you see your loved ones who died in Christ. "You can do it! Keep trusting in Jesus," they shout from heaven. When you feel like quitting, you can hear them calling out to you, "Don't give up now. You're not that far from the finish line."

Can the saints in heaven really see us on earth? I don't know, but Hebrews 12:1 at least allows us to think of them as cheering us on. And that image is part of the communion of saints.

Death cannot separate us from the saints in heaven.

When I was a child, I pictured heaven as somewhere beyond the

175

farthest galaxy, a wonderful land so far away that I would need a rocket ship to get there. Hebrews 12:22-24 offers a different picture, telling us something amazing about what the gospel has done for us.

> *You have come to Mount Zion and to the city of the living God, the heavenly Jerusalem, and to innumerable angels in festal gathering, and to the assembly of the firstborn who are enrolled in heaven, and to God, the judge of all, and to the spirits of the righteous made perfect, and to Jesus, the mediator of a new covenant, and to the sprinkled blood that speaks a better word than the blood of Abel.*

In the original Greek text the phrase "you have come" literally means "you have come near." Once we were far from God, but now in Christ we have come into God's very presence. Once we were faraway, but now we live in the presence of the angels. And now in Christ we have come into the presence of the spirits of righteous men made perfect, a clear reference to believers in heaven.

Think of what he is saying:

• We're not that far from heaven.
• We're not that far from the angels.
• We're not that far from our loved ones in heaven.
• We're not that far from God.
• We're not that far from Jesus himself.

Heaven is a real place, where Jesus is right now, and it's not far away from us. Between us and heaven there is a gossamer veil called death. To us that veil seems dark and forbidding, but in Christ that veil is the portal to our eternal home. Eternity is not visible to us in this life, but it is near us and around us all the time—like the angels surrounding the armies of Israel that Elisha showed to his servant in 2 Kings 6:15-17. The angels were there all the time, but the servant could not see them until his eyes were opened.

Heaven is a real place, where Jesus is right now, and it's not far away from us.

Several of our hymns speak of this aspect of our communion with the saints in heaven. Consider the last verse of "The Church's One Foundation":

> *Yet she on earth hath union*
> *With God the Three in One,*
> *And mystic sweet communion*
> *With those whose rest is won:*
> *O happy ones and holy!*
> *Lord, give us grace that we,*
> *Like them, the meek and lowly,*
> *On high may dwell with thee.*

The great hymn "For All the Saints" speaks to this truth as well:

> *And when the strife is fierce, the warfare long,*
> *Steals on the ear the distant triumph song,*
> *And hearts are brave, again, and arms are strong.*
> *Alleluia, Alleluia!*

What does this mean?

Death cannot destroy our fellowship with the saints of God.

We are one with them, and they are one with us. I do not mean that we can communicate with them. The Bible specifically forbids that. On the TV show *Crossing Over* John Edward seems to receive messages from the dead, but in truth he is deceiving himself and others. "The communion of saints" doesn't refer to ghosts or visions or dreams. The saints of God are alive in heaven while we are alive on earth. They are not that far away from us, and one day we will be reunited with them. They are gone from our sight, but they are not gone from God, and they aren't really gone from us either. As we praise God on earth, they join us in heaven. That is the "mystic sweet communion" the hymn-writer had in mind.

Another verse of "For All the Saints" brings all these strands of truth together:

Credo

O blest communion, fellowship divine!
We feebly struggle, they in glory shine;
All are one in Thee, for all are Thine.
Alleluia, Alleluia!

Theologians sometimes speak of the church militant and the church triumphant. We are the church militant because the battle rages around us every day, and we are called to fight the good fight and take up the whole armor of God. But one day we'll lay our weapons down, and our battles will be over. In that happy day we'll join the church triumphant in heaven. But whether we are on earth today or in heaven tomorrow, we are part of the church of Jesus Christ, "the communion of saints."

THINK ABOUT IT!

1. Do you agree that the gospel transcends race, age, family background, religious affiliation—all human barriers? What does this really mean, and how does this truth manifest itself practically?

2. What is the relationship between communion with God and Christ and communion with other believers on earth? Does one affect the other? Which has to come first?

3. Do you agree that heaven isn't far away from us? What does this mean for the way you live your life? What does it have to do with practical decisions you make day by day?

17

The Positive Power of Forgiveness: "The Forgiveness of Sins"

As far as the east is from the west, so far does [God] remove
our transgressions from us.

PSALM 103:12

If you know a bit about church history, you know that before Martin Luther became the father of the Protestant Reformation, he was a Catholic priest. As part of his training, he spent years studying Greek, Hebrew, Latin, the church fathers, and the doctrine of the Roman Catholic Church. By all accounts he was brilliant, devout, and very devoted to his studies. But his soul was deeply troubled. Burdened with the haunting sense that his sins were not forgiven, he felt that God's judgment hung over him like a heavy weight he could not lift. In desperation, he went to Rome, hoping to find answers, but he came away even more overwhelmed with despair.

Several years later, while studying the book of Romans, he encountered the phrase, "The righteous shall live by faith" (1:17). He now saw clearly that God forgives us not because of anything we do, but solely on the basis of what Jesus did for us when he died on the cross and rose from the dead. So it's not surprising that Luther said the phrase, "I believe in . . . the forgiveness of sins" is the most important article in the Apostles' Creed. "If that is not true, what does it matter whether

179

God is almighty or Jesus Christ was born and died and rose again? It is because these things have a bearing upon my forgiveness that they are important to me."[23]

This phrase summarizes the entire Christian life. That's amazing when you think about how the Apostles' Creed is constructed. The Creed is a God-centered statement of the Christian faith, placing great emphasis on God the Father and the Lord Jesus Christ. The Holy Spirit is mentioned in one brief phrase. Two phrases deal with the church as the fellowship of true believers. But when we come to the realm of the Christian life, it's all summed up in one phrase, a brief seven words: "I believe in . . . the forgiveness of sins."

That's certainly not how we think about things today. Go to just about any Christian bookstore and you'll see a small shelf called "Bible Doctrine" or "Theology," and then you'll see a huge section called "The Christian Life." There you will find books on prayer, growing in faith, enduring hard times, spiritual gifts, spiritual growth, overcoming temptation, sharing your faith, and growing in holiness. There are books on marriage, books for men, books for women, books on the family, raising children, overcoming an addiction, forgiving others, spiritual warfare, singleness, sex, health, the purpose-driven life, and the end times, to name only a few. To us the Christian life is all about these different categories. But the Creed takes the whole Christian life and boils it down to this one essential thing: "I believe in . . . the forgiveness of sins." As if to say, "If your sins are forgiven, everything else is just details. And if your sins are not forgiven, nothing else really matters."

I find that a liberating way to look at the Christian life. I want to ask a question: Are your sins forgiven, and do you know it?

Are your sins forgiven, and do you know it?

We will focus on Psalm 130:3-4 to help us answer three questions about forgiveness.[24]

WHY DO WE NEED FORGIVENESS?

Verse 3 says, "If you, O LORD, should mark iniquities, O Lord, who could stand?" Novelist Franz Kafka wrote in his diary that the problem with modern people is that we feel like sinners, yet have no guilt. We sense that something is amiss in our lives, but we live in a society that tells us to get rid of guilt by getting rid of the rules that make us feel guilty. So we do our best to ignore pesky things like the Ten Commandments. All those "Thou shalt nots" make us nervous.

We try to do away with the rules, but the rules won't go away because they weren't written by man in the first place. Even when we try to ignore or erase them, they keep coming back. We cheat and steal and lust and sleep around, we mock God by killing the unborn and trying to redefine marriage to fit our own twisted desires, but we can't get rid of guilt by pretending the rules aren't there anymore. God has spoken, and he did not stutter. "Thou shalt not" still means "Thou shalt not."

God has spoken, and he did not stutter. "Thou shalt not" still means "Thou shalt not."

Nevertheless we convince ourselves we can ignore the rules and get away with it. That perfectly describes life in Oak Park, Illinois, where I pastor Calvary Memorial Church. Not long ago the village trustees voted to oppose the Federal Marriage Amendment that would define marriage as between a man and a woman. People in Oak Park are against such limitation because they're liberated, they're hip, they're progressive. On matters of sexual freedom, Oak Park has been on the cutting edge of societal evolution for a long time. But men don't make the rules of morality. Village trustees cannot change the truth any more than they can cancel the law of gravity.

That's only one illustration of the larger trend. In today's society, if we don't like a rule, we vote it down or simply say, "I'm going to do whatever I want to do, and no one can stop me." We make up the rules as we go along, hoping true moral guilt will go out the window. But it's never as simple as that. After we relativize the rules and normalize guilt, something is still wrong. Despair, shame, restlessness, and dissatisfaction are rampant. We know something is wrong with us, but we don't know what, and we don't know how to fix it.

Psalm 130 points us in the right direction. This psalm has a long history in Christian tradition. It's titled *De Profundis*, a Latin phrase that means "out of the depths," taken from verse 1: "Out of the depths I cry to you, O LORD." The whole psalm teaches us that we can never fix ourselves because we lack the inner resources to solve our own problems. That flies in the face of Oprah and Dr. Phil and a host of other self-help gurus who say the answer is within us. The Bible says the opposite is true.

The problem is within us. The answer lies outside of us.

As long as we think you can solve our own problems, we will only get worse. But when we finally say, "Lord, please help me. I can't do it on my own," we can receive God's salvation.

Why are we so reticent to confess our sins and receive the forgiveness we need? We're afraid that if we own up to our own stupidity, the Lord will send us straight to hell. So we lie about our lies, and we cover up our cover-ups. We pretend that we didn't do what we know we did. No wonder we're so messed up. Our children learn to make excuses by watching us make excuses. We blame everyone except ourselves.

Psalm 130 liberates us from that self-destructive cycle. Verse 3 teaches that God doesn't keep a record of our sins. But in the Hebrew it literally says that God doesn't keep an eye on our sins. That is, he's not looking for a reason to send us to hell. Many people picture God as a cranky old man who's hoping to catch us messing up so he can send us to the lake of fire. But that's not the God of the Bible. He is willing to forgive those who repent of their sin and cry out for mercy.

Knowing that we are graciously forgiven by the Lord when our works do not fully conform to the law makes us far more prompt to obey, as we find in Psalm 130:4—"with you there is forgiveness; therefore you are feared." (John Calvin, in 1, 2 & 3 JOHN by John Calvin and Matthew Henry)

We need forgiveness because we are sinners who try to change the rules so we can do away with guilt. But since the rules can't really be changed, we end up extremely messed up on the inside. Here is the bottom line:

We need forgiveness, and we cannot live without it.

Without forgiveness, we are hollow men and women, empty and conflicted on the inside. The one piece of good news is that God doesn't keep an eye on our sins if we believe in Christ. If he did, we'd all be in hell already.

WHAT HOPE DO WE HAVE OF FORGIVENESS?

Can we really be forgiven, or is forgiveness just a distant dream? If the Vegas bookies laid odds on our forgiveness, what would the odds be—50,000 to 1, or 100,000 to 1, or maybe even 1,000,000 to 1? Look in the mirror, and consider your own soul. If you do, the outlook will not be hopeful. One British writer put it this way: "There is no man who, if all his secret thoughts were made known, would not deserve hanging a dozen times a day."

"There is no man who, if all his secret thoughts were made known, would not deserve hanging a dozen times a day."

The first part of verse 4 brings us some very good news: "But with you there is forgiveness." Or to say it another way, God makes a habit of forgiving sin. He looks for chances to forgive us because forgiveness is in his nature.

• He is eager to forgive.
• He is ready to forgive.
• He wants to forgive you.

Exodus 34:6-7 calls him "merciful and gracious, slow to anger, and abounding in steadfast love and faithfulness, keeping steadfast love for thousands, forgiving iniquity and transgression and sin."

You need to know that sin is real.

You can't get away with breaking the rules forever. But when you are ready to come clean, the Lord is right there waiting for you. It's never easy to confess your sins, but listen to the invitation God makes in Isaiah 55:7: "Let the wicked forsake his way, and the unrighteous man his thoughts; let him return to the LORD, that he may have compassion on him, and to our God, for he will abundantly pardon." Maybe you don't like that word "wicked" or the word "unrighteous." Maybe that sounds harsh to you. But that's God's description of the whole human race. That's what you and I are apart from God's grace. Don't get hung up on the negative words and miss the invitation. Turn to the Lord, and you will find mercy and pardon.

> **You can't get away with breaking the rules forever. But when you are ready to come clean, the Lord is right there waiting for you.**

Picture two doors, each with two words emblazoned across them:

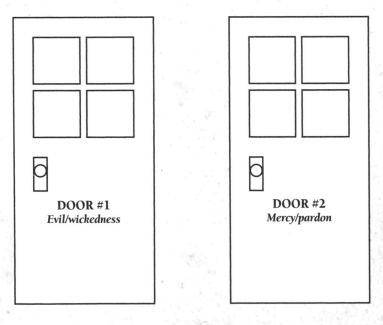

DOOR #1
Evil/wickedness

DOOR #2
Mercy/pardon

Which door do you like better? The answer is obvious: We all prefer mercy and pardon. But God says you have to go through the door marked Evil/wickedness to get to the door marked Mercy/pardon. But someone says, "I'm going to skip Door #1 and go directly to Door #2." It can't be done. If you don't acknowledge your sinfulness, you cannot receive God's forgiveness.

But when you go through Door #2, you discover that God will freely pardon. *Freely* means without cost, no charge. You want mercy? You've got it. You want a pardon for all your sins? You've got it. You can go in evil and wicked, and you can come out with mercy and a full pardon from the Lord. That's the best offer in the world.

WHAT HAPPENS WHEN WE ARE FORGIVEN?

The last part of verse 4 has the answer: "That you may be feared." Another way to say this is, "Therefore we worship you." Once we are forgiven, a vague feeling of unease is removed, our slate is wiped clean, the prison cell door swings open, and we walk out. We're free at last. Sometimes that's the hardest part to accept. Each week I receive letters from prisoners who have read my book *An Anchor for the Soul* and then write to tell me their stories. A man who had committed a particularly heinous crime said he is afraid to go to church because he worries that people will find out what he did and will shun him. That kind of shame works in all of us to keep us in bondage. The devil whispers to us, "You're no good. If people knew what you're really like, they'd have nothing to do with you. You hypocrite."

The only way to deal with Satan's accusations is to go back to the character of God: "With you there is forgiveness." Some Christians fear that when they stand before the Lord he is going to project all their sins on some huge screen for millions to see. They fear that on that day all their ugly words and deeds, all their secret sins that no one else knew about, every dark thought filled with lust, pride, hatred, rage, and greed, will be displayed before the whole universe. How could they endure such a moment? And how could God ever welcome them into his kingdom after putting their depravity on public display?

If you, O Lord, kept a record of sins, if you gazed on our sins, who could stand? No one. We'd all be doomed and damned. But that's the whole point of Psalm 130. We cry from the depths of shame and guilt, and God says, "I have good news for you—with me there is forgiveness." The Bible uses a number of images to describe how God deals with our sins.

- God removes our sins as far as the east is from the west, a distance that cannot be measured (Psalm 103:12).
- God puts our sins behind his back (Isaiah 38:17).
- God blots out our sins like a thick cloud (Isaiah 44:22).
- God forgets our sins and remembers them no more (Jeremiah 31:34).
- God buries our sins in the depths of the sea (Micah 7:19).

When God forgives our sins, he chooses to forget them forever. Our sins are forgiven, removed, buried, and blotted out. They can never condemn us again. But how could God forgive us? Why doesn't he look at or remember our sins?

A long time ago God fixed his gaze on the cross of his Son, the Lord Jesus Christ, who bore our sins.

When we are honest enough to admit that we are wicked and evil, a stream of mercy flows out from the cross of Christ, and our sins are covered by his blood. We discover in one shining moment that with God there is forgiveness.

That's why Luther said this was the most important part of the Apostles' Creed. That's why this is the only part of the Christian life mentioned in the Creed. This is the whole ball game right here; everything else is just details. With God there is forgiveness. That's why the Creed says, "I believe in . . . the forgiveness of sins." Nothing is more important.

THINK ABOUT IT!

1. Do you accept God's laws as binding and true, or do you try to rewrite them in your own mind? Why?

2. Have you accepted God's verdict for your soul? Have you confessed your sins to him and asked for his forgiveness? If not, why not do it now?

3. If you have already received God's pardon, thank him for it now by composing an original prayer of thanksgiving, using some of the analogies of Scripture and some of your own.

18

The Hardest Doctrine to Believe: "The Resurrection of the Body"

*In a moment, in the twinkling of an eye, at the last trumpet
. . . the dead will be raised imperishable, and we shall be
changed. For this perishable body must put on the imperishable, and this mortal body must put on immortality. . . .
then shall come to pass the saying that is written: "Death is
swallowed up in victory." "O death, where is your victory?
O death, where is your sting?"*

1 CORINTHIANS 15:51-52, 54

I believe . . . in the resurrection of the body." That's the hardest phrase in the Creed to believe because it goes against everything we
are taught and everything we see with our eyes. We have lots of funerals, but the last resurrection happened two thousand years ago. And if
you have walked away from the grave of a loved one, you know how
the harsh reality of death can erode your faith. We need to say the Creed
to remind ourselves that we believe death will not have the final victory.

**We need to say the Creed to remind ourselves that we
believe that death will not have the final victory.**

Death is the fundamental human problem and our greatest fear.
Death is so final, so forbidding, so shocking to our senses that we find

it difficult to even say the word. We say that someone "passed on" or "departed" or "slipped away" to soften the blow a bit. I fully understand the need to use euphemisms when a loved one has died. And I believe the funeral industry plays an important role in bringing comfort to grieving families. But even after we have done our best to mask the reality, death stands as a stark reality. The Grim Reaper visits every home sooner or later.

And so we come face to face with a question asked by philosophers, theologians, and especially by grieving families, a question Job asked thousands of years ago: "If a man dies, shall he live again?" (Job 14:14). Consider how Paul faces the same question in 1 Corinthians 15:32: "If the dead are not raised, 'Let us eat and drink for tomorrow we die.'" If the dead are not raised, then why not live it up? Why not go for all the gusto we can? Why bother going to church? Why suffer for Christ if this life is all there is? Why serve the Lord if death ends everything? Down deep in our souls we want to know the truth. When we die, will we live again? Or does death win in the end? If we do not have an answer to death, our religion is useless.

It is precisely at this point that the Apostles' Creed provides positive help. The Creed ends on a very positive note of Christian hope. The penultimate phrase says, "I believe in . . . the resurrection of the body." Note how specific this is. Not "the resurrection of the dead" but "the resurrection of the body." Older versions of the Creed were even more specific, using the phrase "the resurrection of the flesh." Christians believe that the body itself will be raised from the dead. We believe that our redemption will not be complete until the body itself is resurrected from the dead.

Paul wrote extensively about this truth in 1 Corinthians 15, the resurrection chapter.

THE BODIES WE HAVE

Suppose you could instantly change the way you look—would you do it? And would you change just a few things or do a total makeover?

Our bodies wear out. They sag, expand, wrinkle; joints get creaky, arteries harden, gravity pulls everything downward, the heart slows down, eyes grow dim, teeth fall out, arms grow weary. Our bones break, and our muscles weaken. The body bulges in the wrong places. It happens to all of us sooner or later. I ran across an article called "51 Signs You're Getting Older."[25] Years ago I wouldn't have paid any attention to an article like that, but nowadays I find such pieces fascinating. (It helped that the subtitle said, "Large Print Edition.") Here are a few items that caught my attention:

1. Everything hurts and what doesn't hurt doesn't work.
8. You look forward to a dull evening.
11. You sit in a rocking chair and can't get it going.
12. Your knees buckle, and your belt won't.
15. Your back goes out more than you do.
19. You sink your teeth into a steak, and they stay there.
39. You have a dream about prunes.
51. When you bend over, you look for something else to do while you're down there.

As we age, we pay more attention to diet and exercise. As I write this, the Atkins Diet is the rage. Fat and protein are in; carbs are out, way out. (Some feel this is changing, but I doubt the craze will go away.) There is a great variety of low-carb specials, even low-carb ice cream. As far I'm concerned, that's just not right. I eat ice cream because I want the carbs, know what I mean? My wife Marlene, my son Nick, and I saw a sign advertising low-carb pizza. There ought to be a law against stuff like that.

Fitness is in too. There's Weight Watchers and Jenny Craig and Curves and the South Beach diet. We're surrounded with runners and bikers and marathoners and people who like to lift weights four times a week. Fashion is in also. We're very concerned about how we cover our bodies—and in most cases we cover up the parts we don't want anyone else to see because we're out of shape.

Well, I have a bit of news for you. Your body won't last forever. You can eat all the low-carb ice cream you want, but your body will still fall apart in the end. Whether you believe it or not, you're falling apart even while you're reading this book.

Your body is a gift from God that won't last forever.

THE DEATH WE'LL FACE

Most people fear death and don't want to talk about it. Death remains the "final frontier" that we all must cross sooner or later, and though we all know that it's coming, we prefer to live as if it won't. The wonders of modern science help us live longer, but no one can avoid death.

Let dissolution [death] come when it will, it can do the Christian no harm, for it will be but a passage out of a prison into a palace; out of a sea of troubles into a haven of rest; out of a crowd of enemies, to an innumerable company of true, loving, and faithful friends; out of shame, reproach and contempt, into exceeding great and eternal glory. (John Bunyan)

What does the Bible say about death?

- *Death is certain.* "It is appointed for man to die once . . ." (Hebrews 9:27a).
- *Death is not the end.* ". . . and after that comes judgment" (Hebrews 9:27b).
- *Christ defeated death.* "Christ Jesus . . . abolished death and brought life and immortality to light through the gospel" (2 Timothy 1:10).
- *Death remains the final foe.* "The last enemy to be destroyed is death" (1 Corinthians 15:26).

The conundrum for Christians lies between the third and fourth paragraphs. If Christ has abolished death, why do we still die? The answer lies in understanding the basic nature of death. Biblically, the essence of death is separation.

Death is the unnatural separation of the body and the spirit.

That thought runs counter to the current popular notion that death is a "natural" part of life. There is nothing natural about death! It's the most unnatural event in the universe. According to the Bible, death came into the world because of sin (Romans 5:12). When sin has been removed once and for all from the people of God, death will no longer exist for them. That's why there will be no death in heaven (Revelation 21:4). In the truest sense, then, death is unnatural because sin is unnatural. Neither was part of God's plan for us. We can hardly imagine a world where sin no longer exists. But there is such a world, and according to the Bible that world is the real world, while this world that feels so real to us is actually passing away. So until then we live in an unnatural state of affairs where death still stalks our trail. But what is will not always be.

Christ truly destroyed death when he died and rose again, abolishing death as a ruling power in the universe.

Christ truly destroyed death when he died and rose again, abolishing death as a ruling power in the universe. Death itself will one day die (except for those who reject God's offer of forgiveness). Until that day comes, we live in an odd situation best described by Ecclesiastes 12:7: "the dust returns to the earth as it was, and the spirit returns to God who gave it." From a purely human perspective, that is our destiny. Ecclesiastes 12:7 accurately describes what happens when we die, but that verse is not the end of the story.

THE RESURRECTION WE'LL ENJOY

If death is the fundamental human problem (and it is), what is the Christian answer? Listen to Paul's soaring words in 1 Corinthians 15:51-55.

Behold! I tell you a mystery. We shall not all sleep, but we shall all be changed, in a moment, in the twinkling of an eye, at the last trumpet.

> *For the trumpet will sound, and the dead will be raised imperishable, and we shall be changed. For this perishable body must put on the imperishable, and this mortal body must put on immortality. When the perishable puts on the imperishable, and the mortal puts on immortality, then shall come to pass the saying that is written: "Death is swallowed up in victory." "O death, where is your victory? O death, where is your sting?"*

Our coming resurrection will happen instantly. The text says "in a moment, in the twinkling of an eye." One moment the dead will be in the ground; the next moment they will be raised to life. This is no gradual resurrection—if such a thing could be contemplated. The great miracle will happen so fast that if you blink, you will miss it!

It will happen when Jesus returns. "The last trumpet" refers to the return of Christ in the air. The trumpet will sound, the dead in Christ will rise, and living believers will be raptured off the earth to meet the Lord in the air (1 Thessalonians 4:13-18).

It will result in our complete transformation. In that moment our essential being will change from mortal to immortal and from perishable to imperishable. Our individual personalities will remain intact, but all that relates to mortality, death, and decay will be removed from us once and for all.

It is natural to want to know more about the resurrection. The people in Paul's day wanted more information also:

> *But someone will ask, "How are the dead raised? With what kind of body do they come?" You foolish person! What you sow does not come to life unless it dies. And what you sow is not the body that is to be, but a bare kernel, perhaps of wheat or of some other grain.* (1 Corinthians 15:35-37)

Go to your garden if you want to understand the resurrection of Christ. When you grow fruit, you plant the seed in the ground, cover it up, water it, fertilize it, and then leave it alone. Through some process that we cannot observe with our eyes, the seed dies, and out of its death comes new life. Eventually fruit comes forth and is harvested. If you place the seed and the fruit side by side, they look nothing alike, but the seed is necessary for the fruit to appear.

Or hold a tiny acorn in your hand and study it. Suppose that you had never seen an oak tree, and suppose you had no idea what an acorn would produce. Studying an acorn by itself, you would never figure out that it would produce an oak tree. Nothing in the visual inspection would lead you to suspect that such a tiny thing could produce such a magnificent result. But plant the acorn, let it grow, come back in fifty years to see what it has produced, and you will be amazed. From that humble beginning has come an incredible tree, with limbs that stretch in every direction and leaves that provide a vast green canopy.

You would be hard-pressed to imagine that such a mighty tree could come from such a humble beginning. One is so small and insignificant, the other so mighty and impressive. But the acorn contained the mighty oak tree. It was there all along, waiting for the right time and place to come out. How does it happen? The acorn must be planted in the ground and must die before the oak tree can appear. But without the humble acorn, there would be no oak tree at all.

This is the essence of Paul's argument. Today we are humble acorns—just a bunch of nuts! Not much to look at and not very impressive. The day will come when we must die and be planted in the ground. (By the way, when we talk about "planting Uncle Joe" in the ground, that's not just a joke—that's good biblical terminology. We plant Christians in the ground in anticipation of their coming resurrection from the dead.) But that planting is not the end of the story, according to the Bible.

As the acorn dies to produce the mighty oak, even so we die, and our death becomes the gateway to our future resurrection.

We cannot say what the resurrection body will be like with certainty, but it will be to this life as the oak tree is to the acorn.

The resurrection of the body is necessary to reverse the effects of sin.

Old age, disease, accidents, terrible tragedies—these things are all part of the curse upon the earth because of sin. Redemption has to do with the body, not just the soul. Your salvation will not be complete until your body becomes immortal and imperishable.

> Redemption has to do with the body, not just the soul. Your salvation will not be complete until your body becomes immortal and imperishable.

We believe in resurrection, not reincarnation.

If I come back as a Chihuahua, I'll probably just bite someone on the ankle. But I won't come back as someone else or something else. I'll be raised as Ray Pritchard with all the destructive marks of sin removed from all parts of my being. The parts of me that annoy other people will be gone forever, thank God. What remains will be Ray Pritchard, cleansed and purified and perfected by the grace of God. I will still be me, and you will still be you. But we will also be like Jesus because we will see him as he is (1 John 3:1-3). We will have new bodies fit for new people who will live in the New Jerusalem.

After Jesus rose from the dead, the disciples could still recognize him, and he bore on his body the marks of his suffering. He ate and drank with them, and yet he also appeared and disappeared from their midst, suggesting that in his glorified state he transcended time and space.

Your current body is like an old jalopy. It never works very well, it keeps breaking down, and one day it will stop altogether. But your new body will be like a Rolls-Royce that never needs servicing. This is wonderful news for those who today suffer from cancer, deformities, disabilities, sicknesses, chronic illness, and broken body parts. A day is coming when they will suffer and weep no more.

When Christ saves you, every part of you is saved, and every part of you will be delivered from sin. Here is the whole matter in one sentence: It is not *soul* salvation that we believe in, but *whole* salvation. The resurrection of the body is the final step in our salvation.

- Step #1: We are saved from the *penalty* of sin. That happens when we trust Christ.
- Step #2: We are saved from the *power* of sin. That happens day by day through the new life given to us by the power of the Holy Spirit.
- Step #3: We are saved from the *presence* of sin. That will happen in the future when our bodies are raised from the dead and transformed by God's power.

HOW WILL GOD DO IT?

Many people were incinerated on 9/11 when the twin towers of the World Trade Center collapsed. Their bodies simply vaporized. How will God resurrect the bodies of believers who died that day? Or of believers whose bodies were lost at sea or in the jungle? The answer in all cases is the same: The God who holds every molecule of the universe in his hand can retrieve the right ones when the time of resurrection finally arrives. Think of it this way: If you can raise the dead, you can raise the dead. The circumstances of death will not delay or deter the Lord on that great day. Everyone who died a believer will be raised immortal.

Death will not have the last word.

We are "sown in dishonor . . . [and] raised in glory" (1 Corinthians 15:43). "Dishonor" describes our condition at the moment of death because our bodies begin to decay the moment life ebbs away. "Glory" describes what we will be when Christ returns and we are raised from the dead. From dishonor to glory—that's our destiny. How will God do it? Paul says, "I tell you a mystery" (v. 51). The best arguments in favor of resurrection are simple analogies. We are like a little baby in the womb who hears voices from the outside and sees light shining into the womb. We know as much about the resurrection body as that little baby knows about life after birth. What we know is wonderful, but the reality will go far beyond anything we can imagine.

In all of this, we must not miss the great point Paul wishes to make:

Credo

- "O Grave, where is your victory?" It is gone!
- "O Death, where is your sting?" It is gone!

The resurrection of the body means that when God saves us, he saves the whole person—body, soul, and spirit.

If we truly believe what God has said, why should we fear dying? Death has been so thoroughly defeated that for believers the moment of death is the moment of personal victory through Christ their Lord.

Death has been so thoroughly defeated that for believers the moment of death has become the moment of personal victory through Christ their Lord.

What I have written here is not pie-in-the-sky dreaming but sober biblical truth.

We know it is true because it rests on the resurrection of Jesus from the dead. Because he rose, we too shall rise.

When Benjamin Franklin was twenty-three years old, he wrote an epitaph for himself. Though it was not actually used when he died many years later, the epitaph reflects deep spiritual truth:

The body of
Benjamin Franklin, Printer
(Like the Cover of an Old Book
Its Contents torn Out
And Stript of its Lettering and Gilding)
Lies Here, Food for Worms.
But the Work shall not be Lost;
For it will (as he Believ'd) Appear once More
In a New and More Elegant Edition
Revised and Corrected
By the Author.

He was right about that.

We will one day rise from the dead—revised and corrected by the Author himself—never to die again.

Death cannot ultimately touch the person who is joined with Jesus by faith. That is what it means to say, "I believe in the resurrection of the body."

THINK ABOUT IT!

1. What is our culture's attitude generally toward death? What is your attitude toward death? Why? Does it agree with or differ from that of the Bible?

2. Summarize what Scripture has to say about the coming resurrection of believers. What does this mean for you personally?

3. What does the acorn-oak tree analogy mean to you? Do you find this helpful or confusing? Why? What key Scriptures speak to this, and what do they mean to you?

19

We're Not Home Yet: "Life Everlasting"

We know that while we are at home in the body we are away from the Lord, for we walk by faith, not by sight. Yes, we are of good courage, and we would rather be away from the body and at home with the Lord. So whether we are at home or away, we make it our aim to please him.

2 CORINTHIANS 5:6-9

Where is home for you? Recently Marlene and I went to the supermarket to do some shopping. There we saw a woman tapping the watermelons one by one. She tapped and listened and then explained to a friend how you can tell by the sound which watermelons are juicy and sweet. All my life I've heard people talk about doing that, but I've never been able to do it myself. As we turned to walk away, I heard her say to someone else, "I learned that from my grandfather in Alabama." So I turned around and said, "You're from Alabama?" "Yes." "So am I. What part of Alabama are you from?" "Troy." That's in southern Alabama—good watermelon country. I was born and raised at the other end of the state.

Without any prompting from me, she shared a bit of her life story. "I was born in Alabama and lived there for twenty-one years. I've been in Chicago for eighteen years, but I can't get used to it. Too big, too crowded, too many people. Every year I go home to Alabama for a family reunion, but I can't go this year." I could tell she was sad about that. After we went our separate ways, I kept thinking about what she'd said. She's been in Chicago a long time, but she doesn't feel at home here. Home for her is in Alabama. That's where her family is. That's where she's from. She would probably say, "I live in Chicago, but I'm from Alabama." I suppose I feel somewhat the same way.

ALABAMA, MONTANA, OAK PARK

Robert Frost said, "home is where, when you go there, they have to take you in." Oak Park feels like home to me. It hit me recently that I've lived here longer than anywhere I've been except for my growing up years in Alabama. It's been thirty years since I lived in that small town in Alabama, and when I go there, I know lots of people. But there are many more now that I don't know, and they don't know me.

My wife, Marlene, is from Montana. Even though she grew up for the most part in Arizona, Montana is for her what Alabama is for me. It's home, it's where she was born, it's where her people are. My sons Josh and Mark were born in California, and Nick was born in Dallas. But if you ask them where they are from, they'll say Oak Park. This is the town where they grew up. This is for them what Montana is for Marlene and what Alabama is for me. Thirty or forty years from now, they will still come back to this place, to this town, to their own people.

From time to time I meet people who aren't from anywhere. They've lived in so many places that nowhere is home to them. Many of us have also had the experience of going back home, wherever that might be, and finding out that it doesn't feel the way we remember it. I could go back to the small town where I grew up, and I could walk down the main street, and most folks wouldn't recognize me. Even when you go home, it doesn't always feel like home.

And that brings us to the final phrase of the Apostles' Creed: "I believe in . . . life everlasting. Amen."

THE LAST PHRASE OF THE CREED–
"LIFE EVERLASTING"

Hebrews 13:14 says, "For here we have no lasting city, but we seek the city that is to come." The New Living Translation translates the first phrase this way: "This world is not our home." How true that is. Victor Hugo said we spend the first forty years leaving home and the next forty years going home. We are born saying "Hello," and the rest of life on earth is one long good-bye. Friendships come and go; people move into our lives for a while, and then they drift away. We move from house to house, job to job, church to church, and sometimes we even move from spouse to spouse, always searching, hoping for a place where we will finally feel at home. A place where we can relax and be ourselves. Where we don't have to pretend or try hard to impress others. Where we can say, "Ah, this is where I belong."

Heaven Is Where Jesus Is

For the Christian, that place is called heaven. It's a real place, filled with real people. And contrary to popular opinion, it's not really one long, never-ending church service. Far from it. The Bible says that when we get to heaven we will be "at home with the Lord" (2 Corinthians 5:8). What does that mean? Jesus said to the thief on the Cross, "Today you will be with me in Paradise" (Luke 23:43). The essence of heaven is the presence of Jesus.

Heaven is where Jesus is, and when we are in heaven, we will be with him forever.

Several years ago I was in Atlanta for several days for the Christian Booksellers Convention. I called Marlene and left a message on the answering machine saying I was looking forward to coming home. Now I didn't mean that I was looking forward to the house on Wesley Avenue in Oak Park. And when I got home, I didn't hug the drapes and say, "Drapes, I'm glad to see you." And I didn't say to the rug, "Oh, rug, I missed you so much." The house is beautiful, but it is home because the people I love live there. Home to me is where they are, and if they are not there, it doesn't seem like home at all.

The phrase "life everlasting" tells us that our home isn't in this world. Our home is somewhere else. And we will never really be at home in this world because we are constantly saying good-bye to the people we love the most. They leave us, or we leave them. Our children grow up, they leave home, they come back for a visit, and all too soon they leave again. As the years pass, the visits grow more infrequent. If you are looking for a place where you won't have to say good-bye, you won't find it on Planet Earth. You'll have to go somewhere else. The good-byes of this life are meant to make us homesick for heaven.

The good-byes of this life are meant to make us homesick for heaven.

When Jesus prayed in the Upper Room on the night before his crucifixion, he declared, "This is eternal life, that they know you the only true God, and Jesus Christ whom you have sent" (John 17:3). Jesus defines eternal life as knowing God and knowing him, the Lord Jesus Christ.

If you know Jesus, then you already have eternal life.

We think eternal life means living forever. Well, it does mean that, but it means a lot more than that.

Eternal life in its essence is a relationship.

It's not just living for a hundred thousand years and never dying. If you know Jesus, you have "life everlasting" here and now. It begins the moment you believe in him as your Savior, and it continues right on through your death, and it carries you all the way home to heaven.

If you sometimes feel out of place, without roots, detached for whatever reason, take heart—that's how homesickness feels! Your Chief Shepherd is preparing a permanent home for you in heaven, and he is waiting to see you there! (Adrian Rogers, THE LORD IS MY SHEPHERD)

Chasing the Wind

Most of us see heaven as something that will happen a long time from now. So we get busy trying to create a little bit of heaven on earth. But we are disappointed again and again. And even when we are successful, it doesn't last forever. John Eldredge says it rather poignantly: "God must take away the heaven we create, or it will become our hell."[26] There's a whole book in the Bible that explains that thought— Ecclesiastes. Solomon experimented with all that life had to offer: money, sex, possessions, wine, women, song, parties, education, buildings, books, armies, and vast gardens. He dabbled in everything and became the wealthiest man in the world. This was his conclusion: "Vanity of vanities; all is vanity" (Ecclesiastes 1:2, KJV). All his accomplishments amounted to nothing more than chasing the wind. He even says, "I hated life" (Ecclesiastes 2:17). But that's a good thing to say if hating life causes you to turn to God.

Have you ever wondered why so many people have to hit rock bottom before they turn to the Lord? It's not a coincidence—it's how God set things up. We think real life consists in what we own and what we accomplish. But having climbed to the top of the heap, we find even the greatest success leaves us empty on the inside. It takes years and years for some of us to realize this. And you may go through four or five careers and two or three marriages before you figure it all out.

Let me see if I can tie it all together:

- This world is not our true home, and we'll never really feel at home here.
- Nothing in this world can satisfy us ultimately.
- We won't be truly at home until we are with the Lord in heaven.
- Most of us have to learn this the hard way.
- Eternal life begins the moment we believe, not the moment we die.
- Life everlasting and heaven are all about knowing Jesus.
- The phrase "life everlasting" answers both the futility of this life and the mystery of what happens when we die.

Thomas Kelly captured this truth in the last verse of his famous hymn, "Praise the Savior, Ye Who Know Him":

> *Then we shall be where we would be,*
> *Then we shall be what we should be,*
> *Things that are not now, nor could be,*
> *Soon shall be our own.*

THE LAST WORD OF THE CREED–"AMEN"

It's easy to skip the final word of the Creed. For most of us, "Amen" either means "The prayer is over" or "It's time to eat." And when we see it at the end of the Creed, it's like the caboose at the end of the train. To us it simply means that the Creed is now finished. But the writers of the Creed had something more in mind. The word itself comes from the Old Testament and means, "So be it" or "I agree" or "Yes, this is true." It's not a throwaway word. The word "Amen" teaches us three important things.

These things really are true. In that respect, saying Amen is like the President signing a bill after it has passed in the House and the Senate. We say Amen because the Creed is true—and every part of it is true.

> *I believe in God, the Father Almighty—Amen!*
> *the Creator of heaven and earth—Amen!*
> *and in Jesus Christ, his only Son, our Lord—Amen!*
> *who was conceived of the Holy Ghost, born of the Virgin Mary—Amen!*
> *suffered under Pontius Pilate—Amen!*
> *was crucified, died, and was buried—Amen!*
> *He descended into hell—Amen!*
> *The third day he arose again from the dead—Amen!*
> *He ascended into heaven and sits on the right hand of God*
> *the Father Almighty—Amen!*
> *whence he shall come to judge the living and the dead—Amen!*
> *I believe in the Holy Spirit—Amen!*
> *the holy catholic church—Amen!*
> *the communion of saints—Amen!*

the forgiveness of sins—Amen!
the resurrection of the body—Amen!
and life everlasting—Amen!

The Christian church says Amen to the whole Creed and to every part of it because these things really are true.

Truth demands a personal response. It's not enough merely to say or to recite the Creed Sunday after Sunday. You must at some point decide whether or not you actually believe what you are saying. Saying Amen forces you to make a choice.

It's not enough merely to say or to recite the Creed Sunday after Sunday. You must at some point decide whether or not you actually believe what you are saying.

Truth is ultimately wrapped up in Jesus. Did you know that Amen is one of the names of our Lord in the Bible? In Revelation 3:14 he is called "the Amen, the faithful and true witness."

If you say Amen at the end of the Apostles' Creed, you are saying, "Lord, these things are true, and I truly do believe them, and I truly believe in Jesus Christ as my Lord and Savior." Don't say it if you don't mean it. Note that the Creed begins with the phrase "I believe" and ends with "Amen." This is more than a doctrinal statement. It's a declaration of your personal commitment to what the Creed says. Can you say, "I believe" and "Amen" to the Apostles' Creed?

A LAST THOUGHT

We are now finished with the Apostles' Creed. We started with God and ended with life everlasting. In between we touched on all the major doctrines of our faith.

As Christians, we believe more than the Apostles' Creed, but we don't believe less.

This is the irreducible minimum Christians have always believed. The Creed reminds us that Christianity has a doctrinal basis. Although we talk a lot about a personal relationship with Jesus, that's more than a feeling or a personal experience. It's a relationship based on the truth revealed in the Bible. Several years ago I attended the Twenty-fifth Anniversary Banquet of Crossway Books. Part of the evening featured a film clip of the late Francis Schaeffer talking about the importance of standing for the truth in an age of personal peace and affluence. He predicted in the mid-seventies that a time would come when the unthinkable would become thinkable and even acceptable in our society. I was reminded again how great a prophet he really was. Then there was a brief clip of Edith Schaeffer, now in her nineties. In a slow, clear voice she said, "The only thing that matters is truth." She's right about that.

Truth matters. That's why we need to come back to the Apostles' Creed. I know we live in an anti-intellectual age, but truth matters. I realize that in the evangelical movement we have elevated personal experience almost to the level of Scripture itself, but truth matters.

Truth towers over our personal experience and stands in judgment over our personal opinions.

At some point we have to make up our minds. We can't sit on the fence forever. In the first chapter I talked about three frogs sitting on a log. Two decide to jump off. How many are left? All three are left because deciding to jump and actually jumping are two different things. It's time for us to jump off the log and land on the side of God's truth. We owe it to God, to ourselves, and to the world around us to take our stand on the basis of truth. The world will not be moved by a halfhearted commitment to things we don't really believe.

Truth matters. That's why we study and perhaps recite the Apostles' Creed. It doesn't tell us everything we need to know, but it does tell us where we must begin. Make up your mind to stand on the side of truth. In every word and in every action, build your life on the Word of God, be bold about your faith, and keep your eyes on Jesus, knowing that we aren't home yet.

THINK ABOUT IT!

1. Where is home for you? Why? Spiritually, where is or where will be your home? Why?

2. What do you think will be the best part of heaven? Explain.

3. Can you sincerely recite the Apostles' Creed and end with the word "Amen"? Do you really believe all the biblical truths expressed in the Creed? Why or why not? What does this mean for your life practically?

Notes

1. J. Gresham Machen, *Christianity and Liberalism*, www.biblebelievers.com/machen/index.html.

2. Christina Odone, "Some may hate us, but here we stand," *Manchester Guardian Online*, October 28, 2003, www.guardian.co.uk/comment/story/0,3604,1072386,00.html.

3. In preparing this chapter, I have received a great deal of help from the sermon "I Believe" by Peter Barnes, September 12, 1999, www.fpcboulder.org/Sermons/Sermon9-12-99.htm.

4. William Barclay says that the Creed most likely took its earliest form "not long after AD 100, " in *The Apostles' Creed* (Louisville: Westminster John Knox Press, 1998), p. 4.

5. Charles Spurgeon, "Confidence and Concern, " www.spurgeon.org, August 21, 1859.

6. Dana Blanton, "More Believe in God Than in Heaven, " June 18, 2004, www.foxnews.com.

7. *Luther's Little Instruction Book*, www.ccel.org/ccel/luther/smallcat.text.ii.1.html.

8. http://humaniststudies.org/phpBB2/viewtopic.php?p=1293&sid=3c35209a3794ec574416f1fa98fe5b24.

9. John Perry, "Courtly Combatant," *World Magazine*, December 13, 2003; www.worldmag.com/displayarticle.cfm?id=8356.

10. Al Mohler, Crosswalk weblog, January 30, 2004; www.crosswalk.com/news/weblogs/mohler/?cal=go&adate=1%2F30%2F2004.

11. Homily by Pope Benedict XVI in Rome, April 24, 2005. See www.vatican.va/holy_father/benedict_xvi/homilies/2005/documents/hf_ben-xvi_hom_20050424_inizio-pontificato_en.html.

12. J. I. Packer, *Growing in Christ* (Wheaton, Ill.: Crossway Books, 1994), p. 39.

13. For more on these thoughts, see Peter Lewis, *The Glory of Christ* (Chicago: Moody Press, 1997), pp. 155-157.

14. Alistair McGrath, *I Believe* (Downers Grove, Ill.: InterVarsity Press, 1998), p. 55.

15. John Piper, *The Passion of Jesus Christ* (Wheaton, Ill.: Crossway Books, 2004), p. 11.

16. Cited by Rod Dreher, March 3, 2004, http://corner.nationalreview.com/ 04_02_29_corner-archive.asp#026310.

17. W. A. Criswell, "The Keys of Hell and Death, " www.wacriswell.org/ index.cfm/FuseAction/Search.Transcripts/sermon/1559.cfm.

18. James Merritt, "A World Without Easter, " www.crosswalk.org/faith/ pastors/1256544.html.

19. Charles Templeton, *Act of God* (New York: Bantam Books, 1979).

20. Lee Strobel, *The Case for Faith* (Grand Rapids, Mich.: Zondervan, 2000).

21. See Kenneth Alan Daughters, "The Theological Significance of the Ascension, " *Emmaus Journal*, Winter 1994.

22. David Brooks interview with Dick Staub, May 3, 2004, www.christianitytoday.com/ct/2004/118/33.0.html.

23. Cited by Peter Barnes, " "I Believe in the Forgiveness of Sins," February 20, 2000, www.fpcboulder.org/Sermons/Sermon2-20-00.htm.

24. Many of the ideas in this chapter come from a sermon by Scott Hoezee, "Out of the Depths, " September 14, 2003, www.calvincrc.org/sermons/2003/psalm130.html.

25. You can find this list online at www.freemaninstitute.com/getting Older.htm.

26. John Eldredge, *The Journey of Desire*, Chapter 6 (Nashville: Thomas Nelson, 2000).

Special Note

If you would like to contact the author, you can reach him in the following ways:

If you would like to contact the author, you can reach him in the following ways:

By Letter:

Ray Pritchard
1176 Morning Glory Circle
Tupelo, Mississippi 38801

By e-mail: Ray@KeepBelieving.com

Via the Internet: www.KeepBelieving.com

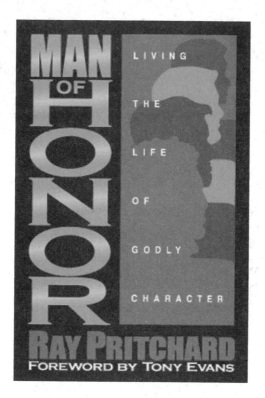

Man of Honor:
Living the Life of Godly Character

The world is in need of men who possess godly character—men who set extraordinary examples in temperament, emotional life, reputation, spiritual life, family life, and personal habits. Do you want to stop living a mediocre life and start being a man of honor for God? This is God's intention for your life, and by his grace you can start anew today!

Any man who is serious about spiritual development will find *Man of Honor* to be a powerful tool. In this book, Pastor Ray Pritchard teaches you to bridge the gap between knowing what the Bible says about godly leadership among men and putting that knowledge into practice.

Questions for personal/group study included

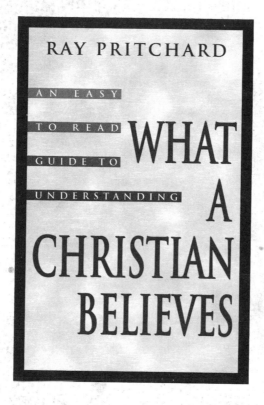

RAY PRITCHARD

AN EASY
TO READ
GUIDE TO
UNDERSTANDING
WHAT
A
CHRISTIAN
BELIEVES

What a Christian Believes:
An Easy to Read Guide to Understanding

What exactly do Christians believe? Is there any proof that God exists? Is the Bible still relevant? How can we know that Jesus is the only way to God?

In this book, Pastor Ray Pritchard covers the core doctrines of Christianity and the reasons underlying those doctrines in user-friendly language—appropriate for those who are unfamiliar with Christianity and for those who practice it but need help articulating their faith. *What a Christian Believes* begins with the thoughtful questions you're asking and concludes with the solid answers you need.

Questions for personal/group study included

Discovering God's Will for Your Life

Life is so unpredictable, and many of us face difficult decisions every day. What is the right thing to do? How do we know God's will for our lives?

Knowing God's will is really about knowing God, and anyone who wants to get to know him, can. Rather than trying to lay out a step-by-step plan for discovering your purpose in life, Pastor Ray Pritchard addresses common questions about God's will and discusses biblical principles on how you can know his plan for you. This insightful book is great for people of all ages and walks of life.

Questions for personal/group study included

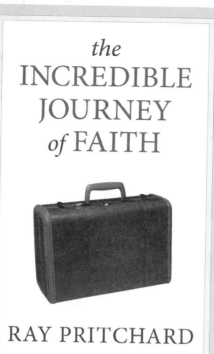

the
INCREDIBLE JOURNEY *of* FAITH

RAY PRITCHARD

The Incredible Journey of Faith

The life of faith is an incredible journey with God that begins the moment we trust Christ and continues until the moment we die. It means accepting God's call without knowing where it will lead, trusting God to keep his promises, and never taking our eyes off of him.

Though we aren't always guaranteed success, comfort, or a trouble-free life, we are promised fellowship with God and assurance of doing his will when we live by faith. Pastor Ray Pritchard reminds us that "to walk with the Lord is the greatest of all joys, and it is indeed safer than a known way." Don't wait—start your incredible journey with God today!

Questions for personal/group study included